CW01497186

# Official Referees' Business

AUSTRALIA AND NEW ZEALAND
The Law Book Company Ltd.
Sydney : Melbourne : Perth

CANADA AND U.S.A.
The Carswell Company Ltd.
Agincourt, Ontario

INDIA
N.M. Tripathi Private Ltd.
Bombay
*and*
Eastern Law House Private Ltd.
Calcutta and Delhi
M.P.P. House
Bangalore

ISRAEL
Steimatzky's Agency Ltd.
Jerusalem : Tel Aviv : Haifa

MALAYSIA : SINGAPORE : BRUNEI
Malayan Law Journal (Pte.) Ltd.
Singapore and Kuala Lumpur

# Official Referees' Business

SECOND EDITION

by

HIS HONOUR
**Edgar Fay,** Q.C.
*of Pembroke College, Cambridge, a Bencher of the Inner Temple, formerly an Official Referee of the Supreme Court*

FOREWORD

by

**The Rt. Hon. Sir John Stephenson**

LONDON
SWEET & MAXWELL

First edition 1983
Second edition 1988


Published in 1988 by
Sweet & Maxwell Limited,
11 New Fetter Lane, London
Computerset by Promenade Graphics Limited, Cheltenham
Printed and bound in Great Britain by
Hazell Watson & Viney Limited
Member of BPCC plc
Aylesbury, Bucks, England



**British Library Cataloguing in Publication Data**
Fay, Edgar
    Official referees business.—2nd ed.
    1. Great Britain. High Court of Justice.
    Official referees' business
    I. Title
    344.203'78624

    ISBN 0–421–39690–3

All rights reserved,
No part of this publication may be
reproduced or transmitted, in any form
or by any means, electronic, mechanical, photocopying,
recording or otherwise, or stored in any retrieval
system of any nature, without the
written permission of the copyright
holder and the publisher, application
for which shall be made to
the publisher.

EDGAR FAY

1988

# Foreword to First Edition

Those who have heard the author of this book present a case against them at the Bar or before them on the Bench would expect him to have made the dullest subject interesting. In this book he has done more than that; he has persuaded one reader to wonder why he ever thought its subject might be dull. I have found very good reading not only in the history of the Official Referees and the development of their business since 1876 but in the practice and procedure so clearly and attractively set out, which will make this an indispensable handbook for all those who decide, or are thinking of deciding, to have their proceedings dealt with, whether directly under the new procedure or by transfer under the old, as "official referees' business."

My first acquaintance with an official referee was unprofessional, when my father introduced me as a boy to an old gentleman who spoke in a hoarse whisper but was able to provide tickets for "the Zoo." This was Sir Edward Pollock, who takes his place in Appendix E below the original four of 1876 and above Sir Frances Newbolt (trimly bearded, like Lord Justice Scrutton, and still officiating as an official referee and Chancellor of the Diocese of Exeter when I was called to the Bar). He had not, when he provided our tickets, completed his 30 years on the Official Referee's Bench doing justice unimpared (I believe) by the handicap resulting from an operation to his throat. I can claim professional acquaintance, and in many cases friendship, with their successors, including the author who is, I am glad to see, one of many judges, and not the last, whom the Inner Temple and the Western Circuit have contributed to the illustrious body now so clumsily designated as "circuit judges nominated by the Lord Chancellor to deal with official referees' business."

How should those judges be described? The old title is today a misnomer, as Mr. Fay points out in his last chapter, for the bulk of the work they now do is specialist construction work which does not come to them by reference under a Master's order or an arbitration agreement. They are now a specialist division of the High Court, and though their pay is less than a High Court judge's, their decisions are in an important respect superior: they cannot be appealed on a question of fact unless it is relevant to a charge of fraud or breach of profesional duty.

They deserve a better name; but Mr. Fay cannot suggest one, nor can I.

Perhaps among the many readers this book deserves will be found one or more who can find a title appropriate to the dignity of the unique office and its business to which Mr. Fay has devoted his time and talents, both as judge and writer, with equal success.

February 1983                                                    John Stephenson

# Preface

Five years ago when I wrote the Preface to the first edition of this book I expressed the hope that it might dispel a little of the air of mystery thought to pervade the official referees' corridor. A great deal has happened since then: the Users' Committee has sprung into vigorous life, the number of permanent judges has been doubled, a new appellate jurisdiction in arbitration has been bestowed, and the Court of Appeal has decided the *Crouch* case. Felicitously, the publication of this edition coincides with the move of the courts to a new home of their own at St. Dunstan's House. Things are moving fast. In 1984 the Attorney-General could speak of the official referees' court as one "about which not much is known." This is no longer true. Thanks largely to the efforts, official and unofficial, of the Users' Committee and its members, the status of the court is beginning to be appreciated beyond its confines. In April 1988 the top Salaries Review Body in its Eleventh Report (Cm. 359) were able to record that "the official referees are required to acquire and develop skills and experience in a highly specialised area of law dealing with issues involving complex technical evidence" and they accepted that "the salary relativity of the London official referees should be raised." And raised it was, to a point rather more than half way between the pay of circuit judges and that of High Court judges. This is progress indeed. Moreover at the Bar Conference of October 1988 a workshop organised by the Official Referees Bar Association is to be devoted to official referees' business. One may now dare to say that the court is emerging from the mists of misunderstanding formerly enveloping it. Perhaps this book has helped. I hope it has.

May I repeat my thanks to all those who assisted me to produce the original work and who are listed in the Preface to the first edition. In addition I now record my gratitude to the many who have helped me to bring the text up to date. They include the senior official referee, Judge Lewis Hawser Q.C., his clerk Mr Richard Carter, Sir William Stabb Q.C., Mr Anthony Thornton Q.C., and, as regards work in the provinces, the Circuit Administrators of each of the circuits and Judge J. A. Stannard and Judge T. R. Heald.

Inner Temple                                                                E. S. F.
June 1988

# Contents

## Part IV: The Future

# Table of Cases

# Table of Statutes

*[All references are to paragraph numbers, those in bold referring
to sections set out in Appendix A]*

# Rules of the Supreme Court

*[All references are to paragraph numbers, those in bold referring to the rule set out in Appendix B]*

# Part I
# The Courts

# Chapter 1
# Introduction: the Court

**The courts**

The official referees' courts in the Supreme Court of Judicature in **1–01**
London are very busy tribunals. About 1,000 cases are brought in to
them each year. Of these less than one-fifth are tried out and the
remainder settle or are otherwise disposed of. Over 4,000 summonses in
interlocutory proceedings are heard in the course of the year. Six to
eight courts sit regularly and at times further courts are called for. The
subject matter of the actions heard in these tribunals is predominantly
construction disputes, and the court has long been recognised as the
specialist tribunal for the trial in the High Court of engineering and
building cases. Many other types of case however find their way to the
official referees' corridor—dilapidations cases, garment industry cases,
commission cases, and matters involving detail or accounting from all
branches of business, commerce and industry. The work has long out-
grown the three purpose-built courts in the west wing of the Royal
Courts of Justice in the Strand and during 1988 the official referees will
be established in their new self-contained home in St. Dunstan's House
in Fetter Lane where eight courtrooms and suitable ancillary accommodation will be available.

**Official referees' business**

Unlike the case of most judicial tribunals there is no section of a stat- **1–02**
ute setting up this court. The court is simply the place where the official
referees are accustomed to sit to exercise their jurisdiction. Official
referees were created by section 82 of the Judicature Act 1873 and were
officially abolished by section 25 of the Courts Act 1971. But the jurisdiction which they exercised prior to the coming into force of that section on January 1, 1972 was preserved and termed "official referees'
business," and by section 25(2) and (3) of the Courts Act:

"(2) Such of the circuit judges as the Lord Chancellor may from

3

time to time determine shall discharge the said functions conferred on official referees.

(3) The cases in which jurisdiction or powers of the High Court or a judge of the High Court may be exercised by official referees, whether by rules of court made under section 15 of the Administration of Justice Act, 1956, or otherwise shall be known as 'official referees' business' and except where the context otherwise requires any reference in any enactment in rules of court or in any other document to an official referee shall, in accordance with this section, be construed as, or where the context requires as including, a reference to a circuit judge discharging the functions of an official referee."

### The Supreme Court Act 1981

1–03    Such was the origin of the term "official referees' business." The above mentioned provisions of the Courts Act 1971, were with effect from January 1, 1982 repealed[1] and replaced by section 68 of the Supreme Court Act 1981. Subsection (1)(a) of this section enacts that rules of court may provide for the cases in which the jurisdiction of the High Court may be exercised by such of the circuit judges as the Lord Chancellor may from time to time nominate to deal with official referees' business,[2] and by subsections (6) and (7):

"(6) The cases in which jurisdiction of the High Court may be exercised by circuit judges nominated under subsection (1)(a) shall be known as 'official referees' business;' and, subject to rules of court, the distribution of official referees' business among judges so nominated shall be determined in accordance with directions given by the Lord Chancellor.

(7) Any reference to an official referee in any enactment, however passed, or in rules of court or any other instrument or document, whenever made, shall, unless the context otherwise requires, be construed as, or (where the context requires) as including, a reference to a circuit judge nominated under subsection (1)(a)."

### The judges

1–04    The three pre-Courts Act official referees were determined by the Lord Chancellor to continue to do official referees' business, and when vacancies have subsequently occurred the Lord Chancellor has appointed persons to be circuit judges and has assigned them at once to official referees' business, so that the continuity and institution of full-

---

[1] Supreme Court Act 1981, s.152(4) and Sched. 7.
[2] For full text of s. 68, see Appendix A below.

time "official referees" has been preserved.[3] Strictly the judges should be referred to as "circuit judges nominated by the Lord Chancellor to do official referees' business"; however when the official referees were seemingly abolished in 1971 the learned editors of *The Supreme Court Practice* surmised that the three circuit judges designated to do official referees' business would continue to be known in popular parlance as official referees, and so it has proved—indeed they may now be said officially to be so called since they have been so termed in post-1971 amendments to the Rules of the Supreme Court. The name "official referee" will be used in this work to refer to post-Act as well as to pre-Act judges doing official referees' business. During the last decade their numbers have been increased and the establishment now stands at six.

### Statutory jurisdiction

In order to ascertain the jurisdiction of the court it is therefore necess-   **1–05**
ary to look firstly at the powers conferred by statute on the official refer-
ees. These powers, save as to arbitration, are all contained in the Rules of the Supreme Court. The enabling statute at the time of the making of the present rules and of the enactment of the Courts Act 1971, was sec-tion 15(1) of the Administration of Justice Act 1956.[4] As from January 1, 1982 that section was repealed and replaced by the slightly different and perhaps wider terms of section 68(1) of the Supreme Court Act 1981.[5] The relevant rules, made under the 1956 Act, and continued in force by the 1981 Act, are to be found in Orders 36 and 37, while ancillary pro-visions are scattered through the rules in paragraphs collected in Appendix B, below. Order 36 was radically amended with effect from October 1, 1982 by the Rules of the Supreme Court (Amendment No. 2) Order 1982.[6] Prior to that date there were two rules, rules 1 and 2, deal-ing respectively with the transfer of cases or issues to the official refer-ees for trial and with the transfer of questions or issues of fact to the official referees for inquiry and report. Rule 2 (reference for inquiry and report) remains unaltered, although re-numbered as rule 8, but rule 1 has been replaced by three new rules. Paragraph (1) of rule 1 applies the Rules of the Supreme Court generally to official referees' business and

---

[3] This applies to London, where the bulk of the work is done. Provincial official referees, created after the Courts Act 1971, was passed, are part-time. See further Chap. 15, below.
[4] s.15(1): "Rules of court may prescribe cases in which the jurisdiction or powers of the High Court or a judge of the High Court may be exercised by official referees or special referees."
[5] Appendix A, para. A–01 below.
[6] S.I. 1982 No. 1111 (L.23).

paragraph (2) of rule 1 goes on to define official referees' business in the following terms:

> "(2). In this Order official referees' business includes, without prejudice to any right to a trial with a jury, any cause or matter commenced in the Chancery Division or Queen's Bench Division, being a cause or matter—
>
> (a) which involves a prolonged examinaton of documents or accounts, or a technical scientific or local investigation such as could more conveniently be conducted by an official referee; or
>
> (b) for which trial by an official referee is desirable in the interests of one or more of the parties on grounds of expedition economy or convenience or otherwise."

Rule 2, which was wholly new and represented a radical alteration in the procedure, authorises a party to mark his writ or originating summons with the words "official referees' business" and "on the issue of the writ or summons so marked, the cause or matter begun thereby shall be treated as "official referees' business." A case may thus now be commenced in the official referees' court; hitherto it had to start elsewhere and be transferred by order to it from the parent Division.

The new rule 3 deals with transfer. It replaces the old rule 1 under which virtually all proceedings had reached the official referees by transfer from the Chancery or Queen's Bench Divisions. The new rule continued this power but introduced a new power enabling the official referee to transfer a case the other way. This is no doubt a corollary to the litigant's right to start his case in the official referee' court. Another novelty was the power now given both to the court and to the official referees to transfer a case of its or their own motion.

Order 37, rule 4 confers jurisdiction upon the official referees to asesss damages. This is a referred jurisdiction. Rule 4 of that Order provides that where judgment is given in the Chancery Division or the Queen's Bench Division for damages to be assessed the Court may order that the assessment of damages be referred to an official referee.

It is to be noted that the jurisdiction of the official referees is defined in very general terms. It is limited to Chancery and Queen's Bench cases, but any case appropriate to those Divisions may be started in or transferred to the official referees' court if so to do is "desirable . . . on grounds of expedition, economy or convenience or otherwise." Some clue as to what is "desirable" is afforded by the words of sub-paragraph (a) of the definition, "a prolonged investigation of documents or accounts, or a technical scientific or local investigation"; but this does not purport to be an exhaustive definition, and the bounds of the jurisdiction are to be found not so much in the definiton as in the practice which has grown up during the century or more of the court's existence.

This practice cannot be fully understood without looking at the origin and history of the official referees and their courts. These are dealt with in the next three succeeding chapters, and the jurisdiction as it is found in practice is further considered at paragraphs 6–01 and 6–02, below.

### Characteristics

Official referees' business presents certain important differences in **1–06** procedure from ordinary trials in the Chancery or Queen's Bench Divisions. These peculiar characteristics are:

(1) Cases are, from their entry in the official referees' department, assigned by rota to a named judge.[7]
(2) The judge to whom the case is assigned himself hears and decides interlocutory applications.
(3) Interlocutory appeals go straight to the Court of Appeal.
(4) There is no appeal on questions of fact from a decision of an official referee except in cases of fraud or professional negligence.

A fifth characteristic, of great importance a century ago but no longer cogent, is that there can be no jury trial of an official referee's case.

To these statutory characteristics there must be added two points of practice. The first is that the London official referees will sit to hear the whole or part of a substantial case in any part of the country if the litigants wish it. The second is that the judges operate what might be termed a limited dossier system: in advance of interlocutory proceedings they expect to be provided with the relevant papers and to familiarise themselves with the issues; in consequence they not infrequently themselves make suggestions with a view to rendering the trial more manageable or shorter or less expensive.

### Official referees' business in the provinces

Prior to the amendments to the law made by the Courts Act 1971, the **1–07** three (or at times four) official referees based in London attended to all official referees' business in England and Wales, sitting in London or outside as seemed convenient. As will be shown later[8] one of the wants they were created to fulfil was to provide judges who were not tied to London or to infrequent assizes, but who would sit wherever the parties wanted. Under the powers conferred upon him firstly by section 25(2) of the Courts Act 1971, and now by section 68(6) of the Supreme Court Act 1981, the Lord Chancellor has assigned the London official referees to the south-eastern circuit and has also designated certain of

---

[7] Except in the provinces; See Chap. 15.
[8] See para. 2–05 below.

the circuit judges on each of the other circuits to do official referees' business. While the London or south-eastern circuit official referees are employed full-time on official referees' business, the provincial judges are part-time official referees. Litigants in the provinces, except in the south-eastern circuit, have the option of going before their local judge or of entering their case in London. And whether or not a case comes from a provincial district registry the London official referees are still empowered to sit, and do sit, not only in towns on the south-eastern circuit but also anywhere in England and Wales which is convenient to the parties. This subject is more fully dealt with in Chapter 15, below.

### Official referees as arbitrators

1–08    As will be seen in the next chapter, the original conception of the official referees as arbitrators to whom parts of cases were referred derived from the practice of arbitration and linked the early official referees with arbitrators. A survival of this link exists in the provisions of section 11 of the Arbitration Act 1950, (re-enacting section 3 of the Arbitration Act 1889) that an official referee must act as arbitrator in any private arbitration in which he is called upon so to do. This is an original jurisdiction; arbitrations come direct to them and are not referred by order of a court or judge.[9]

### Literature

1–09    Official referees have received scant attention from the authors and editors of legal text books. The only comprehensive account of their history and operations is the article entitled "Official Referees" by the late Sir Roland Burrows Q.C. at 56 L.Q.R. 504. A useful account of their practice is contained in the introduction to the title "Referees" in Atkin's *Court Forms*[10]; this is edited, among others, by the then senior official referee. Reference may also be made to the notes to Order 36 in the current *Supreme Court Practice*. There is a useful chapter on official referees' business in R. Fenwick Elliott, *Building Contract Litigation*. For law reports see paragraph 13–10 below.

---

[9] The subject of arbitrations by official referees is dealt with in Chap. 20 below.
[10] Vol. 33, 1981 issue, pp. 269 *et seq.*

# Chapter 2
# The Origin of Official Referees

## A Victorian problem

The mid-nineteenth century was a time of general dissatisfaction **2–01** with the modes of trial of civil litigation in England. In the common law courts all questions whether simple or complex were tried by jury. In the Chancery courts the convoluted procedures pilloried by Charles Dickens still prevailed. The rivalry, and sometimes antagonism between law and equity passed from inconvenience to abuse. Some relief had been afforded by the setting up of county courts in 1846, but those courts' jurisdiction was originally limited to claims for debt or damage not exceeding £20 and if the claim exceeded £5 either party was entitled to require trial by jury. The litigation of commerce and industry was untouched and businessmen in all departments of commercial life continued to labour under the delays and quirks of an outmoded legal system—and to complain bitterly of the expense, the delay, the uncertainties and, in the case of provincial litigants, of the concentration of business in London.

## Arbitration

Businessmen did more than complain. In increasing numbers they **2–02** withdrew their custom from the courts in favour of arbitration. There is no statistical evidence recording the number of arbitrations year by year, but it is evident that as the nineteenth century progressed more and more trades began as a matter of course to embody arbitration clauses in their contracts. They thus avoided the law's delays and technicalities, although as time went on it became apparent that the practice of arbitration itself was developing quirks and injustices of its own. By mid-century the courts and the legal establishment had become sufficiently aware of the problem to set about considering how to improve

9

what would today be termed legal services. The first timid attempt to improve the service afforded by the courts to the businessman can be discerned in the provisions of the Common Law Procedure Act 1854. This for the first time permitted a common law judge to try a question of fact without a jury, although the utility of the innovation was diminished by the provision that trial by judge alone could only take place if all the parties agreed and the judge consented.

### The seed: compulsory arbitration

2–03    It had long been apparent that some issues of fact of a scientific or technical or detailed nature could not satisfactorily be tried by a jury. Nor were the common law judges, unaccustomed to deciding civil disputes without the aid of a jury, noticeably willing to assume the burden of such matters. Unless there existed an enforceable arbitration agreement, they had no power to require parties to resort to arbitration, although it seems that judicial pressure was sometimes exerted to procure the parties' consent to arbitration, and some use was made, particularly in the Court of Chancery, of the device of referring technical matters to an expert, with the parties' consent. What was needed, it came to be thought, was the power to divert such questions compulsorily, when they arose in the course of litigation, into the hands of an arbitrator, who would decide them informally, in private, locally where necessary, and freed from the shackles of contemporary legal procedure. This viewpoint found its first expression in the same Common Law Procedure Act of 1854, section 3 of which read as follows:

> "If it be made to appear at any time after the issuing of the writ to the satisfaction of the court or a judge upon the application of either party that the matter in dispute consists wholly or in part of matters of mere account which cannot conveniently be tried in the ordinary way it shall be lawful for such court or judge upon such application if they or he think fit . . . to order that such matters either wholly or in part be referred to an arbitrator appointed by the parties or to an officer of the court . . . and the award or certificate of such referee shall be enforceable by the same process as the finding of a judge upon the matter referred."[1]

The "officers of the court" were the Masters but the arbitrator was an innovation, a compulsory referee within the litigation process. Here in this tentative step, confined one feels somewhat apologetically to

---

[1] "The draftsmen of the 1854 Act had in mind two precedents: the practice of the Court of Chancery of ordering reference to officers of the court or specially qualified persons to inquire and report, and the other the practice of making consent orders for arbitration." Burrows, "Official Referees," 56 L.Q.R. 510.

"matters of mere account" was sown the seed of the official referees' courts.[2]

## The Royal Commission of 1867

The Common Law Procedure Act 1854 seems to have had little effect **2–04** in stemming the commercial community's flight from the law courts. But the habits of the court's rivals, the arbitrators, were coming under increasing criticism also. They charged large fees; they sat when they pleased and adjourned when they had other business to attend to; they disregarded the principles of natural justice and could only rarely be called to account if they erred in law: such was the indictment against them. However they were still regarded as a lesser evil than ordeal by litigation: as was said at a later date by an eminent authority, "the mercantile public is not fond of law, if law can be avoided. They prefer even the hazardous and mysterious chances of arbitration in which some arbitrator who knows as much of law as he does of theology, by the application of a rough and ready moral consciousness, or upon the affable principle of dividing the victory equally between both sides, decides intricate questions of law and fact with equal ease."[3]

Against this background the government in 1867 took the major step of appointing a Royal Commission headed by Lord Cairns, then a Judge of Appeal in Chancery and soon to become Lord Chancellor, to consider what was to be done about the judicature. This was of course the Commission whose report led to the sweeping away of the old courts of common law and equity and to their replacement by one Supreme Court with its Court of Appeal and its High Court whose Divisions afforded some continuity with the past. These fruits of their labours are known to every law student; what is less generally remembered is that in their first Report, the one which led to the root-and-branch Judicature Act 1873, they isolated two problems as standing in the forefront of their task, the first problem being the evils of the duel system of equity and common law and the second being how to try complex issues of fact.

## The Judicature Commissioner's Report

Upon the second of these problems the Judicature Commissioners **2–05** had this to say:

"It has long been apparent in the practice of the courts of common

---

[2] "It was this extended use made of this system of arbitration by the courts which induced the Judicature Commissioners to recommend, and the Judicature Act to create, the office of official referees."—Holdsworth, *History of English Law*, Vol. XIV, p. 198.

[3] Anonymous article on the Judicature Acts, said to be by Lord Bowen, *The Times*, August 10, 1892.

law that there are several classes of cases litigated in those courts to which trial by jury is not adapted and in which the parties are compelled—in many cases after they have incurred all the expense of a trial—to resort to private arbitration. Until the Common Law Procedure Act of 1854 the parties could not be compelled to go to arbitration, and the power given by that Act is limited to cases where the dispute relates wholly or in part to matters of mere account or where the parties have themselves before action agreed in writing to refer the matter in difference to arbitration."[4]

The Commissioners went on to record that arbitrators fell into two classes; they were either barristers or experts. The barristers, they found, were unable owing to the calls of their practices to give continuous attention to a case, and the experts, they found, owing to lack of legal training, were wont to entertain irrelevant considerations and to deal unsatisfactorily with legal questions. Fees were large, adjournments were frequent, and erroneous results could not be put right by appeal. The Report continues:

"It seems to us that it is the duty of the country to provide tribunals adapted to the trial of all classes of cases and capable of adjusting the rights of litigant parties in the manner most suitable to the nature of the questions to be tried.

We therefore recommend that great discretion should be given to the Supreme Court as to the mode of trial and that any question to be tried should be capable of being tried in any Division of the court—

(1) by a judge
(2) by a jury
(3) by a referee."[5]

The Commission then gave their recommendation in the following terms:

"We think there should be attached to the Supreme Court officers to be called Official Referees and that a judge should have the power at any time after the writ of summons and with or without pleadings and generally upon such terms as he may think fit to order a cause, or any matter arising therein, to be tried by a Referee; and that whenever a cause is to be tried by a Referee such trial should be by one of these Official Referees unless the judge otherwise orders. . . . The judge should have power to direct where the trial shall take place and the Referee should be at

<hr />

[4] First Report of the Judicature Commissioners, March 25, 1869, 25 Parliamentary Papers 1868/69 (No. 41340), p. 12.
[5] *Ibid.* p. 13.

liberty . . . to adjourn the trial to any place which he may deem to be more convenient. The Referee should, unless the judge otherwise directs, proceed with the trial in open court *de die in diem*."[6]

The Commission thus wished to incorporate compulsorily into litigation the process of arbitration but shorn of its disadvantages of expense, lack of continuous sitting, and lack of appeal on law. The good was to be taken, the bad rejected. As *The Times* newspaper said in a leading article a few years later "the office of official referee was one of the most striking novelties of the Judicature Act 1873."[7]

### The Judicature Act 1873

The Royal Commission had been appointed on September 18, 1867. **2–06** Its first Report was dated March 25, 1869. Its recommendations were adopted, and on August 5, 1873 the grand Judicature Act received the Royal Assent. The new Supreme Court of Judicature was created, and by section 83:

> "There shall be attached to the Supreme Court permanent officers to be called Official Referees for the trial of such questions as shall under the provisions of this Act be directed to be tried by such Referees. . . . Such Official Referees shall perform the duties entrusted to them in such places, whether in London or in the country, as may from time to time be directed or authorised . . . and all such proper and reasonable travelling expenses incurred by them in the discharge of their duties shall be paid by the Treasury out of moneys to be provided by Parliament."

The functions of these new judicial creatures were set out in sections 56 and 57 of the Act:
Section 56:

> "Subject to any rules of court and to such right as may now exist to have any particular cases submitted to the verdict of a jury, any question arising in any cause or matter (other than a criminal proceeding by the Crown) before the High Court of Justice or before the Court of Appeal may be referred by the court or by any Divisional Court or judge before whom such cause or matter may be pending, for inquiry and report to any official or special referee and the report of such referee may be adopted wholly or partially by the court and may (if so adopted) be enforced as a judgment of the court . . ."

---

[6] *Ibid.* pp. 13–14.
[7] *The Times*, May 29, 1876.

Section 57:

> "In any cause or matter (other than a criminal proceeding by the Crown) before the said High Court in which all parties interested who are under no disability consent thereto, and also without such consent in any such cause or matter requiring any prolonged examination of documents or accounts, or any scientific or local investigation which cannot in the opinion of the court or a judge conveniently be made before a jury or conducted by the court through its other ordinary officers, the court or judge may at any time on such terms as may be thought proper, order any question or issue of fact or any question of account arising therein to be tried either before an official referee, to be appointed as hereinafter provided, or before a special referee to be agreed on between the parties . . ."

### Delay in implementation

2–07    The Judicature Act 1873, came into force on November 2, 1874, but 12 months later no official referees had yet been appointed. The delay caused some disquiet, and in its issue of November 13, 1875 the *Law Times* wrote with reference to the official referees "since the clauses giving power to make such appointments are some of the clauses of the Judicature Act from which considerable practical advantage may reasonably be expected to be derived, it seems somewhat desirable to call public attention to the fact that they have not yet been put into operation."[8] The newspaper had high hopes of such appointments. The article continued by expounding the still existing evils and the relief which the appointment of official referees would give in the following terms:

> "The consequence of the defects of the present system is that in cases of moment in this at present inevitable delay the parties have hitherto generally preferred appointing and paying an arbitrator selected by themselves to having their cases heard by the Masters of the courts. Now the proposed system of the appointment of official referees seems admirably adopted to supplement the weak points of the present system and to provide reasonably speedy cheap and efficient tribunals. If men of standing and practical experience in whom the parties can have confidence are appointed and compelled where the parties require it to hold sittings in the

---

[8] (1875) 60 L.T. 30.

place where the question in dispute arises or where the parties and their witnesses reside, one of the chief objections to the present references before Masters is met, and if their sittings are held *de die in diem*, as the Act contemplates, another great objection to the present system, that of the delay consequent on the matter being referred to a Master, is also obviated. The sittings of the official referees *de die in diem* will also tend, apart from any question of expense, to make a trial before one of them a more favourite mode of trial than a reference to an arbitrator chosen by the parties; unless indeed such arbitrators abandon their present usual methods of proceeding which consists of adjourning from time to time as may suit their own convenience or that of counsel on either side."[9]

## The first official referees

The *Law Times* article, stressing the need for official referees "of high 2–08 standing and acknowledged ability," advocated the formation of a panel of eminent practitioners who would be part-time referees and from the list of whom the parties would be allowed to select their judge. This was not a plan to commend itself to the authorities. In an unhurried fashion they eventually selected four barristers, two of them silks, to be full-time official referees, and their appointment was announced to the House of Commons by the Home Secretary on February 15, 1876.[10] They were James Anderson Q.C., George Dowdeswell Q.C., Charles Roupell, barrister-at-law, and Henry Verey, barrister-at-law. These four pioneers entered upon a statutory framework which has in outline remained to this day (although, as will be seen, the practice has altered greatly in the intervening century). They were to sit continuously, sit wherever was convenient to the parties, and decide matters without the aid of a jury. Their decisions were to be of two kinds: they either held an inquiry under section 56 and reported back to the judge, or they tried an issue or issues under section 57 and made a finding equivalent to that of a jury. In the latter case the cause or matter still had to go back to the judge for the rest of the case to be tried, or, if all the issues had been referred, for the judgment to be given. Their status was ill-defined but clearly they were subordinate to the High Court judiciary. In one important respect the recommendations of the Judicature Commissioners had not been carried into the Act: they were not given authority to try the whole of a case or to enter final judgment.

[9] (1875) 60 L.T. 30.
[10] (1876) 62 L.T. 310.

### Special referees

**2–09**    By its references to special referees the Judicature Act brought forward and gave statutory force to the old practice of referring technical questions to experts agreed upon by the parties. The office of special referee has lingered in the statute book until the present day, but little or no use is now made of them and this work does not deal with the practice or procedure of special referees.

# Chapter 3
# Early History

**An inauspicious start**

Despite the high hopes held out for the innovation of arbitration **3–01** within the litigation process, the immediate results were disappointing. This was due to three factors. First, the Judicature Act had failed to confer on the new official referees jurisdiction to try the whole of a case, as recommended by the Royal Commission; the limitation of their powers to trying parts of cases tended to diminish their status in the judicial hierarchy. Secondly, the scale of fees laid down for the provision of their services unimaginatively followed the practice of arbitrators and tended to discourage recourse to the new system. The fees were one guinea per hour of sitting time and in the case of sittings outside London the plaintiff was required to provide a suitable hall at his own expense, to pay the official referees an extra one and a half guineas per night, and to defray "the reasonable costs of their locomotion."[1] Thus one of the reasons for setting up the new referees—the securing of trial at a place convenient to the parties—was rendered particularly expensive. The third factor was the identity of the first four appointees. In a leading article on November 27, 1875 expressing the hope of speedy implementation of the official referee provisions the *Solicitors Journal* had said "to do justice to suitors and to make the scheme a success the official referees ought to be chosen from the best men at the bar. The salary of £1,500 which it is understood the Treasury are prepared to offer to the four official referees to be appointed is certainly inadequate."[2] When three months later the appointments were announced it became clear that the authorities had taken a more modest view of the qualifications required for the office. They did pay a little more, namely £1,700, but the identity of the appointees drew a storm of criticism.

[1] (1875) 20 S.J. 380.
[2] (1875) 20 S.J. 70.

17

### The storm

3–02    To say that the first four appointees were not well received by the profession would be an understatement. The *Solicitors Journal* said they "cast no lustre upon the office" and termed one in particular "a bad appointment."[3] A correspondent signing himself "Not a Candidate" said "it is quite beyond hope that the very respectable old gentlemen and the very inexperienced young one who have been appointed can possibly satisfy the requirements of suitors."[4] The profession seems to have been affronted. The *Law Times* said "the outcry against the proposed appointment of the gentlemen selected to fill the office of official referee ought to open the eyes of the government to the mistaken policy which has been adopted by them. It is evident that men of greater reputation than any of the gentlemen ominated (with the exception perhaps of Mr. Dowdeswell Q.C.) are clearly required both by the public and the profession."[5]

### The Commons debates

3–03    The prevailing dismay was soon reflected in Parliament. On March 10, 1876 in the House of Commons in Committee of Supply a reduction in the Supreme Court vote was moved in order to draw attention to what Sir Henry James M.P. called "a grave and important scandal." The move seems to have taken the government by surprise and the debate was postponed. It was resumed on May 26, 1876 when the method of selection of the official referees by the Lord Chancellor was explained to the House. Apparently Mr. Anderson Q.C. was the Lord Chancellor's own appointment: he was described by Lord Cairns as "a gentleman of long standing, high reputation and considerable practice at the Bar." The names of Mr. Dowdeswell Q.C. and Mr. Roupell had been put forward by Lord Coleridge, then Chief Justice of the Common Pleas and later Lord Chief Justice of England. Mr. Verey had been proposed by the Lord Chief Baron. The Lord Chancellor, it was said, had had the highest reports of all of them. It was upon the last named that the attack then became concentrated. It appeared that he was counsel of 10 years call whose main professional experience had been in the now long since abolished office of "revising barrister" for Parliamentary elections, an appointment which he also owed to the Lord Chief Baron. On the one hand he was described as a briefless and unknown young man whose appointment was a scandal; on the other hand he was said to be "a gentleman of considerable attainments although he had not enjoyed the

---

[3] (1875) 20 S.J. 289.
[4] (1875) 20 S.J. 296.
[5] (1876) 60 L.T. 354.

smiles of the attorneys."[6] It was conceded that he had never held a brief; on the other hand it appeared that solicitors in whose offices he had worked before call to the Bar had constantly had the benefit of his opinions. After a lengthy debate the vote was passed but the publicity hardly enhanced the standing of the new court. *The Times* devoted a leader to the affair, saying in characteristically pontifical style:

> "It seems to be established now that the office was not filled hastily or recklessly but with a very good consideration of its character and that Mr. Verey was accepted on the grounds of special personal qualifications which outweighed his comparative deficiency in practice. If the precedent is dangerous the inquiry which has followed is a proof that such exceptional appointments are held to be specially brought under the notice of Parliament."[7]

By way of footnote it may be recorded that Mr. Verey remained quietly at his work from 1876 to 1920, retiring aged 83 after 44 years in office. This exceptionally long service was recognised at his retirement by the conferment of a knighthood on the advice of Lord Chancellor Birkenhead. He died in the same year.[8]

## Further complaints

Once the House of Commons had appraised itself of the state of the **3–04** new official referees it continued to keep an eye on them. It managed to secure the reform of the fee system. The Attorney-General (Sir John Holker) had been quick to point out in the May 1876 debate that the hourly fees went into the Consolidated Fund and not into the official referees' pockets. In the following July,[9] he answered a question about the fees by saying that as yet there had been too slight an experience of the working of the system to say whether a modification of the practice should be introduced or not. By the next February however, when there was a debate on delays in the new Supreme Court of Judicature he acknowledged that the official referees were making little contribution to shifting the work and by now he thought the fee system might be to blame: "It had been expected that a very considerable amount of relief would be afforded by the appointment of referees . . . it had happened however that they had not had much work to do and the reason might be that they were authorised to charge a certain fee per hour before sitting and that this had been distasteful and perhaps unjust to suitors . . .

---

[6] *Hansard*, 3rd series, Vol. 222, col. 1315.
[7] *The Times*, May 29, 1876.
[8] Sir Henry Verey's 44 years is thought to be a record in modern times for judicial longevity: the runner-up is Lord Denning with 42 years.
[9] *Hansard*, 3rd series, Vol. 230, col. 817.

he had come to the conclusion that if the fees were diminished or abolished recourse might be more frequently had to the referees."[10]

### Fee system reformed

3–05    The Attorney-General's prognostication proved correct. The hourly fee was abolished in favour of the system which has prevailed down to the present day, a nominal fee per case, then £5, now £30. It seems to have made all the difference, despite the poor opinion held of the office holders. In 1880 there was another debate in the House of Commons. Mr. Rylands, the member for Burnley, perhaps wishing to harass the government, moved to reduce the Supreme Court vote by £6,800, the salary of the four official referees. He claimed that their work was so light that there was no public necessity for their appointment or at any rate that their numbers might be reduced from four to two without prejudice to the administration of the law; Mr. Verey, for example had sat on only 59 days in the legal year 1877/78.[11] Replying, the Solicitor General (Sir Farrer Herschell) conceded that there had been ground for criticism on account of the small amount of work done by the official referees for their salaries. But, he said, this state of things had now entirely changed. He outlined the old and new fee systems and said that before the change in the fee structure, rather than go to official referees the parties used to go to special referees whom they appointed and whom of course they had to pay. But that was in the past: "during the present year the four official referees had been fully occupied, almost all of them having sat on every day during the legal year except in the vacations and some having been unable to get through the amount of work provided for them. . . . In consequence of the amount of work which now came before the official referees it would be impossible to dispense with the services of any one of them without causing delay to the discharge of business."[12] A legal member confirmed that they were now giving "entire satisfaction," and the member for Burnley withdrew his motion.[13] The House of Commons did not again turn its attention to the official referees until 1984.[14]

### Jurisdiction extended

3–06    Once the official referees' courts began to be adequately used in the early 1880s the desirability became apparent of doing what the Royal Commission had envisaged and entrusting to them the trial of the whole of a case. At first this enlarged jurisdiction was timidly limited to

[10] *Hansard*, 3d series, Vol. 232, col. 979.
[11] *Hansard*, 3rd series, Vol. 255, col. 694.
[12] *Hansard*, 3rd series, Vol. 255, col. 697.
[13] *Hansard*, 3rd series, Vol. 255, col. 698.
[14] See para. 4–08 below.

20

cases where both parties consented. By section 9 of the Supreme Court of Judicature Act 1884:

> "In any cause or matter (other than a criminal proceeding by the Crown) now pending or hereafter commenced before the High Court of Justice or Court of Appeal in which all parties who are under no disability consent thereto the Court or a judge may at any time, on such terms as may be thought proper, order the whole cause or matter to be tried before an official referee who shall have power to direct in what manner the judgment of the Court shall be entered and to exercise the same discretion as to costs as the Court or judge could have exercised."

### The definitive jurisdiction

The restriction to cases where the parties agree was soon removed. **3–07** The Arbitration Act 1889 repealed the earlier provisions and by section 14 codified the official referees' trial jurisdiction in terms which governed their work for seven decades and which set up the mould which, though repealed, still influences what is properly to be described as official referees' business.

> "In any cause or matter (other than a criminal proceeding by the Crown)
> (*a*) if all the parties interested who are not under disability consent: or
> (*b*) if the cause or matter requires any prolonged examination of documents or any scientific or local investigation which cannot in the opinion of the Court or a judge conveniently be made before a jury or conducted by the Court through its other ordinary officers or
> (*c*) if the question in dispute consists wholly or in part of matters of account:
> the Court or a judge may at any time order the whole cause or matter, or any question or issue of fact arising therein to be tried before a special referee or arbitrator respectively agreed on by the parties or before an official referee or officer of the Court."

The alternative procedure of inquiry and report[15] was brought forward by section 13 of this Act, replacing section 56 of the Judicature Act 1873.

### The court in the nineties

By 1890 the framework for official referees' business had thus reached **3–08** a recognisably modern pattern. At the start the official referees had operated it seems from their several chambers, but in 1892 they had

---

[15] See para. 2–06 above and para. 4–04 below.

been given premises of their own in Portugal Street, behind the new Royal Courts of Justice in the Strand. They had plenty of work, although their reputation remained doubtful. Those were the days of patronage, and this on occasion had curious results. The authorities, it seemed, were not yet disposed to heed the lesson of the uproar caused by the first appointments. Certainly the next two appointments added little lustre to the office. These were G. W. Hemming Q.C., appointed in 1877, and Sir Edward Ridley, appointed in 1886. Ridley was the only official referee to have been promoted to the High Court bench, but he owed both appointments to being the brother of a leading politician, Sir Matthew Ridley, Financial Secretary to the Treasury in Lord Salisbury's first administration (1885–6) and later Home Secretary. Those versed in legal literature will be able to call to mind many examples of his ineptitude as a judge. As for Mr. Hemming, he is less well remembered, but vivid accounts of his eccentricities survive. He is portrayed in the late Gilchrist Alexander's *The Temple of the Nineties* as follows:

> "There was another official referee in Portugal Street—one Hemming Q.C.—who it was said had been a senior wrangler and was a very able man. As an official referee he was so bad that nobody would let his case get into his list if he could possibly help it. I used to see him driving up to Portugal Street in a four-wheel cab and shuffle out of it in his carpet slippers and vanish into his room. He was always trying to get work to do and if he succeeded in getting a summons or a case into his list he kept it going as long as he could."[16]

There is also an illuminating glimpse of Hemming in *Reminiscences of a K.C.* by a forgotten silk named Thomas Edward Crispe:

> "Daily he [Hemming] had to listen to things which he did not understand, but he was always determined to master them; if he could not comprehend he got irritable and angry with the witness or counsel who failed to make him understand. The result was an inordinate amount of time wasted . . . He was rude to a degree but he was one of the best fellows alive and his awards were seldom upset. I got on very well with him . . . Under protest from my opponent I often, unsolicited, went on to the referee's platform, and with my hand familiarly on his shoulder solved his difficulties as to a plan and its sections or disposed of the intricacies in accounts or measurements."[17]

---

[16] Gilchrist Alexander, *The Temple of the Nineties* (1938), p. 102.
[17] T. E. Crispe, *Reminiscences of a K.C.* (1909), p. 126.

# Chapter 4
# The Twentieth Century

### Development of the court

By the turn of the century the work of the court was moving towards **4–01** the pattern it exhibits today. Of the two alternative procedures—trial of the action or of issues, and reference and report—the latter had lost popularity as the advantages in speed and cost of the other procedure had become apparent.[1] Building cases were already the staple work of the court. The progress from the informality of arbitration towards the formality of the courts had begun. It seems that robes were worn by both official referees and counsel but counsel remained seated while addressing the court.[2] When this practice was abandoned is not known. It also seems from references in contemporary reports that many proceedings which today would be heard in open court were then dealt with in chambers.[3] In 1897 upon the promotion of Sir Edward Ridley to the High Court, his place was taken by Mr. Edward Pollock, an appointment which met with general approval and may be said to have initiated the process of developing the status of the official referees towards their present standing. Sir Edward Pollock (he was knighted in 1922) took the appointment at an early age because of some affliction of his voice, and he guided the destiny of the court for 30 years. The judicial strength had been reduced from four to three in 1889 and from 1920 to 1927 the three were Sir Edward Pollock, Sir Francis Newbolt, and Mr. G. A. Scott, the inventor of the Scott Schedule. By the time of this triumvirate the stature and reputation of the official referees may be said to have emerged from the unfortunate cloud which clung about their earlier years. In 1940 Sir Roland Burrows was able to write of the official referees "they commenced as subordinate officers and have developed into judges of important actions. . . . The official referees are

---

[1] See Chap. 19 below.

[2] "Official Referees" by Sir Roland Burrows, (1940) 56 L.Q.R. 509.

[3] *e.g.* see the reference to trial in a private room in *Leigh* v. *Brooks* (1877) 5 Ch.D. 592, cited at para. 6–05 below.

23

no longer merely assessing damages where liability has been decided or taking accounts but are now trying a large number of non-jury actions and doing the same work as a High Court judge in such cases. This change has been brought about gradually and successfully and it seems likely as time goes on that more and more actions will be referred to them for trial."[4]

### Growth of the work

**4–02**     Examination of the Judicial Statistics shows that by 1910 the pattern of work had been reached which has continued without alteration to the present day: very few cases for inquiry and report or for arbitration and the majority of cases connected with buildings or engineering works. The number of cases remitted has fluctuated. Between 200 and 300 were brought in annually down to the 1914 war. During that war the number declined but a post-war peak of 507 was reached in 1921. After 1922 the figures drifted back below 300. They passed 400 in 1949, peaked at 465 in 1951, and then dropped back again until recent years. They passed 400 again in 1970 and as the Table at Appendix F shows[5] have exhibited a remarkable increase in the last decade, passing the 1,000 mark in 1985.

### Progress in the twentieth century

**4–03**     From the 1920s onwards the courts of the official referees have been gradually, very gradually, accorded greater jurisdiction, status, and, one may perhaps add, respect. The disposition to entrust them with increasingly important work has been more noticeable in the legislature than among the higher judiciary. The feeling that really important cases should not be tried by an official referee, exemplified in *Leigh* v. *Brooks*[6] no doubt stemmed from the scandals of the early appointments, but some vestiges of this attitude persisted into the twentieth century. However when in 1942 the House of Lords decided[7] that official referees ahould not try cases of alleged professional negligence because there was no right of appeal on fact, Parliament promptly conferred a right of appeal in such cases, and negligence actions against architects, engineers and surveyors became, and remain, a major section of official referees' work. From being arbitrators concerned with part only of a case the official referees gradually become fully fledged judges. Thus by the Administration of Justice Act 1932, appeals were no longer to be by case stated as in arbitrations (or, in interlocutory appeals, to a judge in

---

[4] (1940) 56 L.Q.R. 506 at 512.
[5] See Appendix F, para. F–01 below.
[6] (1877) 5 Ch.D.; see para. 6–05 below.
[7] In *Osenton & Co.* v. *Johnston* [1942] A.C. 130; see para. 6–05 below.

chambers) but were to go direct to the Court of Appeal; in 1938 their personal status was enhanced by their being given by Royal Warrant the style and title of "His Honour" and accorded place and precedence next after knights bachelor; and several further important steps towards their present position were associated with the Evershed Report. Finally in 1982 the right was given to litigants to start their actions in the official referees' court. By thus achieving an original jurisdiction their court may be said to have come of age. The judges were at last not wholly "referees" but were now judges of a specialised court within the High Court, a tribunal comparable in status with the Commercial Court.

## The Evershed Report

The Committee on Supreme Court Practice and Procedure (the **4–04** "Evershed Committee") looked at the official referees' courts in the course of their deliberations in the early 1950s. The then increasing importance of these courts they described as follows.

> "In recent years the ambit of the matters referred to official referees has greatly increased and today a large variety of matters are tried before them, in particular heavy and complicated cases involving matters of detail, *e.g.* cases arising out of building contracts, claims for possession of leasehold premises upon forfeiture for breach of covenant to repair and damages for breach, and claims for commission where a servant or agent is remunerated by commission."[8]

In consequence of the view which they had thus formed, they said:

> "We are satisfied that in these and other special types of cases there may be considerable advantage to the litigant in having the matter referred to an official referee. The hearing is less formal and, due to the great experience of the official referees in the special types of case usually heard by them, more expeditious. Further, in necessary cases the official referee sits outside London in some court or room conveniently near the subject matter of the dispute so that a great saving of costs is achieved where there are a number of local witnesses."[9]

The Committee noted the increasing use being made of the court, necessitating the increase in the number of official referees from three to four which had taken place in 1948, and they felt the jurisdiction to remit cases to them should be widened. This jurisdiction was then

[8] Final Report of the Committee on Supreme Court Practice and Procedure, 1953 (Cmd. 8878) para. 102.
[9] *Ibid.* para. 103.

contained in sections 88 and 89 of the Supreme Court of Judicature Act 1925, which had brought forward the terms of section 13 and 14 of the Arbitration Act 1889, reproduced above.[10] They recommended that the limitation, apart from consent cases, to prolonged examination of documents and scientific and local investigations and accounts, should be dropped and a general power given to remit whenever desirable on the grounds of convenience, economy, expedition or otherwise.[11] This reform was duly carried out, but a modified version of the old formula was reintroduced when R.S.C., Order 36 was amended in 1982. Meanwhile the old form of words had set a practice which is still generally followed.[12] The Committee also made a recommendation which they regarded as a matter of administrative convenience but which in the differing circumstances prevailing today is working a fundamental change in the character of the court. This related to the question of transfer from one official referee to another. They said "We desire to draw attention to the fact that cases are now allotted to the official referees in rotation, except in the cases when parties ask for a particular referee. Once a case has been assigned, it can only be transferred by consent of the parties or by order of the Lord Chancellor. This sometimes results in one official referee having too much work and another having no work at all. Accordingly, we recommend that it be made possible to transfer cases between official referees without the present restrictions".[13] The recommendation was adopted, and the power to transfer has been widely used during the last decade when the official referees' courts have come under increasing pressure.[14]

### Later history

**4–05**     The enhanced status which the Evershed Committee felt the official referees should enjoy was recognised in the provisions of the ensuing Administration of Justice Act 1956. By section 9 of that Act official referees were to be appointed by the Crown on the recommendation of the Lord Chancellor and they were for the first time required to take the judicial oath on appointment; also their duration of office was changed from being as determined by the Lord Chancellor, to being subject only to a retiring age of 72.[15] This Act, by section 15 also enlarged their jurisdiction as proposed by the Evershed Report and transferred the relevant provisions into the Rules of the Supreme Court. When those new rules

[10] See para. 3–07 above.
[11] Final Report of the Committee on Supreme Court Practice and Procedure, 1953 (Cmd. 8878), paras. 107, 108.
[12] This subject is amplified at paras. 5–05 and 5–06 below.
[13] First Interim Report of the Committee on Supreme Court Practice and Procedure, 1944 (Cmd. 7764), para. 108.
[14] See para. 13–02 below.
[15] Extendable to 75 under the Courts Act 1971, s.17(2).

were made the opportunity was taken to sever another link with the original arbitration pattern: the right of the parties, if agreed, to choose their referee was withdrawn, and all cases were in future to be allocated by rota.[16] One matter which the Committee had glanced at was not however dealt with. This was the title of the office. The Committee had said:

> "The official referees . . . made a number of suggestions which seemed to us worthy of consideration but outside the terms of reference of the Committee. Principal among such suggestions was the desire for a change of name from 'Official Referee'. We agree that the title is not very satisfactory and a title which was more appropriate would be an advantage."[17]

The title remained unaltered until its formal abolition by the Courts Act 1971, but the provisions of that Act did at least confer the style of "judge" upon those who had been acting as judges for so long.

The official referees' numbers were reduced from four to three in 1956 and remained at that figure until 1983 when a fourth was appointed. They have moved house more than once. They had moved in 1900 from Portugal Street to the west wing of the Royal Courts of Justice. When great pressure on space in that building developed after the last war they were moved in 1965 to Victory House in Kingsway, but in 1969 they returned to the Royal Courts of Justice, to two courts on the second floor and one on the third floor of the west wing. In 1975 two new courts were constructed for them on the third floor, and for a short time the official referees were compactly and adequately housed. For recent developments see paragraph 4–08 below.

### The Royal Commission and the Courts Act

When the Beeching Report was published in 1970 it was found, to the surprise of some, that the Royal Commission on Assizes and Quarter Sessions had recommended that the official referees should become circuit judges. Their reason for this recommendation was that the official referees helped out with other High Court work. They said:     **4–06**

> "In addition to dealing with their normal work, official referees give valuable help in other ways, for example by sitting as Commissioners of Assize. We see considerable advantage in this, both because of the judicial assistance which it provides, and because of

---

[16] This was the effect of the new Order 36A, introduced on October 1, 1957, giving effect to s.15 of the Administration of Justice Act 1956.

[17] Cmd. 8878, para. 112, *cf.* comment on this paragraph at (1951) 101 L.J. 169; "The description 'official referee' fails to convey to the public any adequate appreciation of the duties and status of the office." However the L.J. could think of no better alternative than "Assistant Justice."

the merit that we attach to variety in the work of all members of the bench. In order that full advantage may be taken of this, we recommend that, while retaining their existing titles, official referees should become members of the circuit bench. This will enible them to help with released High Court cases and, where appropriate, with middle band and released upper band criminal offences. If they did not become members of the circuit bench the only way in which they could give help outside their normal range of work would be by their appointment from time to time as temporary High Court or circuit judges, a method which . . . should only be used in emergency."[18]

The Report also recommended an expansion of the official referees' services outside London,[19] a subject dealt with in Chapter 15 below, "Provincial Official Referees." The ensuing Courts Act 1971, followed the Royal Commission's recommendation in turning the official referees into circuit judges, but did not follow the recommendation that they retain their existing titles.

### Effect of the Courts Act

**4–07**     Technically the office of official referee was abolished at midnight on December 31, 1971 after a life of 98 years. But the business of the official referees was preserved as outlined in Chapter 1 above[20] and the Lord Chancellor's Department has kept alive the institution of the official referee by assigning circuit judges permanently to the work transacted in and from London. Their status is recognised in their pay, which is at a level above that of other circuit judges[21] and the title "official referee," so explicitly abolished by the Courts Act[22] has been preserved in popular parlance and has crept back into official usage. Outwardly the coming into force of the Courts Act made no discernible difference in the practice and the work of the court. It has however had two important practical results. One is to create provincial official referees, operating in those parts of England and Wales beyond the South Eastern circuit. Provincial official referees are taking an increasing share in the workload: cases remitted to them now exceed 500 per annum.[23] And because official referees' business may now be transacted by such circuit judges as the Lord Chancellor may nominate, it is now open to the Lord Chan-

---

[18] Report of the Royal Commission on Assizes and Quarter Sessions, 1969 (Cmnd. 4153), para. 420.
[19] *Ibid.* para. 419.
[20] See para. 1–02 above.
[21] *cf.* Review Body of Top Salaries, Report No. 10, 1978 (Cmnd. 7253), para. 64. Report No. 11, April 1988, (Cmd. 359) recommended a further increase in pay relativity.
[22] s.25(1) and Sched. 2, para. 1(2).
[23] See para. 15–04n below.

cellor to appoint another circuit judge or deputy circuit judge or recorder to try a particular case or to sit for a determined period.

The most recent chapter in this long legislative history was written in 1982, when Order 36 was substantially amended. The provisions of the rules are considered in detail in Chapters 6 and 7 below but what must be mentioned here as an historical landmark is the fact that since 1982 litigants have for the first time had direct access to the official referees' courts and are now freed from the necessity of obtaining an order from a judge or Master of the Chancery or Queen's Bench Divison remitting the case.

## Changes in the 1980s

By 1983 the pressure of rapidly increasing work was threatening the efficiency of the official referees' courts.[24] The belated appointment of a fourth official referee in 1983 did no more than restore the establishment to its size a century earlier. Despite the appointment of deputies to man further courts the interval between writ and trial became longer and longer, and when the long awaited trial date arrived it sometimes happened that no judge was available to sit. Increasing criticism led first to the setting up of the Official Referees' Users' Committee[25] and, channelled by that committee, to protests in the press and, in 1984, in Parliament. On March 30 in that year the debate on the adjournment was devoted to this topic. Mr. Sydney Chapman, the member for Barnet, put forward three proposals, first that the number of official referees should, as a matter of urgency, be increased to six; secondly that they should be accorded the status of High Court judges; and thirdly that better court facilities should be provided. From the legal point of view, he said, the construction industry was "sorely discriminated against in the determination of disputes."[26] In reply Sir Michael Havers, Att.-Gen. (as he then was) announced that the first point was to be met: the Lord Chancellor had authorised an increase in the establishment to six, although that figure would be reviewed when the next retirement of an official referee occurred.[27] The other two proposals were not met: there were no plans for altering the status of the official referees, and accommodation was a problem, shared with other parts of the High Court, which was being looked into.[28]

Four years later the accommodation problem is about to be met. In the rearrangement now planned for all constituents of the Supreme

4–08

---

[24] "The delays in disposing of business before the official referees are, through no fault of theirs, wholly unacceptable": Donaldson M.R. in February 1984, in *Northern Regional Health Authority* v. *Derek Crouch Construction Co. Ltd.* [1984] Q.B. 644 at 674.

[25] See para. 16–01 below.

[26] *Hansard*, 6th series, Vol. 57, Col. 623–625.

[27] *Ibid.* Col. 626–627.

[28] *Ibid.* Col. 628.

Court the official referees are to move in 1988 into self-contained quarters in St Dunstan's House in Fetter Lane.

Another significant event in this period was the formation in 1983 of the Official Referees' Bar Association "to represent the interests of its members and promote the standing and efficiency of the official referees' courts."

# Chapter 5
# The Court Today[1]

## Location

At the present time the London official referees have their own courts   **5–01**
situated on the third floor of the west wing of the Royal Courts of Justice
in the Strand. However, in 1988 the official referees will move to new
and more convenient quarters at St Dunstan's House in Fetter Lane, off
Fleet Street and close to the Mitre Court entrance to The Temple. Normally eight courts will be sitting, six staffed by the permanent official
referees and two more by recorders or deputies.

## Sitting

From Monday to Thursday the courts normally sit in court as   **5–02**
chambers at 10 a.m. or earlier for the despatch of short interlocutory
business. Solicitors and their clerks have audience at the hearing of
summonses, and robes are not worn. At 10.30 the courts are opened,
and the judge sits, robed, for the hearing of whatever case is listed for
the day. Fridays are devoted to originating and other long summonses,
many of considerable length. Thus for trials the court ordinarily works a
four-day week. For trials the judge wears silk's robes and a judicial wig,
as in the Chancery Division. The courts ordinarily rise at 4.15 p.m.
Audience is restricted to counsel, who appear robed and address the
court standing. Litigants in person may of course be heard but a company or other corporation may only appear by counsel.[2] There is now
little discernible difference between the trial of actions and issues in
these courts and similar trials before a Queen's Bench judge, save that a
slightly greater degree of informality may be thought to prevail. Witnesses, unless their evidence is to be short, are invited to be seated.

---

[1] This chapter relates only to the London official referees. For provincial official referees,
see Chap. 15 below.
[2] As a matter of grace, officers of impecunious companies have been permitted to appear
in chambers. On one occasion the impossibility of hearing an officer of a company as
advocate in open court was overcome by the parties agreeing to transform the case into
an arbitration and proceeding accordingly; see Chap. 20 below.

### Sittings outside London

5–03    The London official referees will in appropriate cases sit outside London, both in towns on the south-eastern circuit (the circuit to which they are formally assigned) and also in any other part of England and Wales.[3] See *per* Forbes J. in *Durston* v. *O'Keefe*[4]:

> "Notwithstanding these last appointments [of provincial official referees] the circuit judges taking the official referees' business in London, whom I might call the 'old' official referees, are still available to deal with such business outside London if it is referred to them."

This practice continues one of the features for which the official referees were brought into existence.[5] Arrangements for such sittings are made by the judge's clerk after venue has been decided,[6] and the expense is borne by the Treasury. In practice the court room is found by the appropriate circuit administrator's office and is ordinarily a local Crown Court, although where a sitting is fixed in a town with no Crown Court some other hall or courtroom may be pressed into service. For sittings by provincial official referees, see Chapter 15 below.

### Terms

5–04    The official referees' courts observe the High Court terms as laid down by Order 64, rule 1 and applied by rule 6(1),[7] but of late years owing to pressure of work business has been taken in parts of the long vacation, and also sometimes in the Christmas, Easter and Whitsun vacations. This process has been facilitated by the fact that official referees appointed since the coming into effect of the Courts Act 1971, are expected to sit for the number of days in the year appropriate to circuit judges. During vacations one official referee sits on one day each week for the despatch of interlocutory business.

### Jurisdiction

5–05    From 1888 to 1956 the classes of cases which could form official referees business were governed firstly by sections 13 and 14 of the Arbitration Act 1889,[8] and secondly by the identical terms of sections 88 and 89 of the Supreme Court of Judicature (Consolidation) Act 1925. In 1956 those provisions were replaced by section 15(1) of the Administration of

---

[3] *cf.* Ord. 36, r. 4(3).
[4] [1974] 1 W.L.R. 775 at 777.
[5] See paras. 2–05 and 2–06 above.
[6] See para. 13–04 below.
[7] See Appendix B below.
[8] See para. 3–07 above.

Justice Act 1956[9] which transferred the detailed provisions from the statute book to the Rules of the Supreme Court. (Since January 1, 1982 the enabling provision has been section 68 of the Supreme Court Act 1981). Those rules were amended from time to time and have been substantially amended and partly recast as from October 1, 1982.[10] The rules are in very general terms, the only strict limitation being to cases in the Chancery and Queen's Bench Divisions, thus excluding Family Division matters but including Admiralty matters. So far as the rules are concerned any case in the Chancery or Queen's Bench Divisions may be dealt with if it is consdered desirable in the interests of the parties or of one of them so to do, the only limitation on what is considered to be desirable appearing in the words "on the grounds of expedition, economy or convenience, or otherwise." But the practice regarding what matters were considered to be suitable for transfer was settled by the formula first devised in 1889 and part of the statute law until 1956, and partially reintroduced in the 1982 amendments, where it appears as a sub-paragraph (*a*) of rule 1(2) of Order 36.[11] Examination of this rule shows that the work transferable includes:

(1) cases requiring prolonged examination of documents;
(2) cases requiring prolonged examination of accounts;
(3) cases requiring a technical or scientific investigation;
(4) cases requiring local investigation.

Although supplemented by the more general provisions of Order 36, rule 1(2)(*b*), those categories represent a settled practice which still largely prevails. To these there must now be added a further category, provided for by Order 37, rule 4(1)(*a*)[12]:

(5) the assessment of damages after an interlocutory judgment.

### Principal jurisdiction

Heads (1), (2) and (3) above account for most of the official referees' 5–06 work. The majority of their cases are disputes in the construction and engineering fields where both a wealth of documentary evidence and a conflict of expert opinion are commonly to be found. A substantial minority of cases involves expert witnesses from other fields and commercial cases other than construction ones. Use is still from time to time made of the official referees for local investigation; thus in 1976 a Chancery Division case was tried by a London official referee in a town in west Wales where the numerous witnesses resided. Similarly rights of

[9] See above, para. 1–05, n. 4.
[10] See para. 1–05 above.
[11] See Appendix B below.
[12] See para. 1–05 above.

way cases, where the recollection of elderly local inhabitants was drawn upon, were often tried locally by official referees. The question of what is and what is not considered to be official referees' business is further dealt with in Chapter 6 below.

### Miscellaneous jurisdictions

5–07    The official referees retain their original jurisdiction in private arbitrations, a matter dealt with in Chapter 20 below.[13] They also retain their jurisdiction to inquire and report as opposed to giving judgment. This jurisdiction is obsolescent but while Order 36, rule 8 remains unrevoked it cannot be said to be dead, and the subject is therefore dealt with in Chapter 19 below. Assessment of damages after a judgment has been entered is a separate jurisdiction covered in Chapter 18 below.

### Issues

5–08    Today the greater part of an official referees' court time is employed in trying cases in a manner indistinguishable from the trial of like cases in the Queen's Bench Division. But a considerable slice of their time is spent in trying issues. This is one of the devices stemming from the inception of the office and it comes about sometimes because it is an issue which was the subject of an order to remit[14] or more often because the official referee and the parties find it advantageous to split up a long case into separate parts. Not infrequently an official referee will order trial of "all issues save quantum of damages"; the reasons for such a course and the topic of issues generally are dealt with in paragraph 12–09 below.

### Personnel

5–09    The official referees are circuit judges whom the Lord Chancellor has nominated to deal with official referees' business.[15] The qualification for the office is that of circuit judge, *i.e.* barrister of at least ten years standing or a recorder who has held office for at least five years.[16] The pre-1971 official referees had their own place in the table of precedence[17]; the London official referees now rank at the head of the circuit judges, preceded only by the Vice Chancellor of the County Palatine of Lancaster. They receive a salary between that of circuit judges and that of High Court judges. The senior official referee is *primus inter pares*: he supervises the administration of the official referees' department but

[13] See also para. 1–08 above.
[14] See para. 7–05 below.
[15] Supreme Court Act 1981, s.68(1)(*a*).
[16] Courts Act 1971, s.16(3).
[17] See para. 4–03 above.

receives no extra pay. Each of the judges has a clerk and an usher permanently assigned to him. The clerk has threefold duties: he acts as associate when the court is sitting; he manages the business of his court, including the listing of future cases; and he runs the office for the issue of summonses and the transaction of other business with litigants and their solicitors. The clerk to the senior official referee also coordinates the work of the court as a whole and acts as secretary to the Users' Committee. Since 1981 the court has had a rota clerk whose principal duties are to receive and document incoming cases and to enter them in the rota book in the rotation required by Order 36, rule 5(3), and to issue summonses.

## Registry

It is understood that on completion of the move to St. Dunstan's **5–10** House a Registry will be instituted for the official referees' courts at that address. In the new Registry writs will be issued, notices of intention to defend given, judgments entered and fees paid. Additional staff will be provided.[18]

---

[18] Official Referees' Users' Committee, second Report (May 1988) para. 6.3.

# Part II
# The Practice

# Chapter 6
# Jurisdiction

## Commencement

There are two methods of bringing proceedings before the official **6–01** referees. By the new procedure introduced in October 1982 a litigant may start in the official referees' court by endorsing his writ or originating summons in the Chancery or Queen's Bench Divisions with the words "official referees' business." Under the other procedure, formerly the only procedure, a case started in either the Chancery or Queen's Bench Divisions may be transferred from its parent division to the official referees' court. The detail of the procedure in both cases is dealt with in the next chapter. In either process, it is only those cases which can properly be described as official referees' business which should be so begun or transferred. If a litigant has wrongly begun his case in the official referees' court it may be transferred back to the parent division either on the application of the other party or by an official referee of his own motion.

## What is official referees' business?

Whether a case is or is not official referees' business is of importance **6–02** to the parties because of the differences between the treatment of a case in the official referees' courts and its treatment in the ordinary lists of the Chancery or Queen's Bench Divisions. The differences are set out at paragraph 1–06 above; the most important in practice is the absence of a right of appeal on fact from an official referee's decision (other than in cases of fraud or professional negligence). There is also a major difference in that, because it is the judge who deals with interlocutory matters in the official referees' courts, interlocutory appeals go direct to the Court of Appeal, thus eliminating the stage of appeal from a Master to a judge in chambers—this may be especially relevant in Order 14 cases. The practice in obtaining fixed dates for trial also differs as between the two systems, while length of waiting time between summons for directions and trial may also vary.

### The definition

6–03     From time to time the classes of case deemed to be fit for the official referees' courts have had varying statutory definitions. The central core of the definitions has been complexity and technicality. The original definition in the Judicature Act 1873,[1] gave way after the Evershed Committee's report to a simplified formula of desirability in the interests of expedition, economy or convenience or otherwise.[2] The former definition, in an abbreviated form, has been reintroduced by the 1982 rules as an addition to the Evershed formula—no doubt as a guide to the litigant when considering whether or not to use the new direct procedure. The text of the rule as it now stands is set out at paragraph 1–05, above and see also paragraph 5–06. It will be noted that the definition is in very general terms, is not exclusive, and gives a wide discretion. In the result what is or is not to be deemed official referees' business is largely a matter of the practice as it has developed over the years. Not all matters requiring scientific or technical investigation are included: those controversies of medical science arising in personal injuries cases are not official referees' business. Nor are all cases involving the prolonged examination of documents included: those falling within the definition of "commercial action" in Order 72[3] are appropriate to the Commercial Court and not to the official referees' courts, although the Commercial Court does sometimes remit to the official referees the trial of issues of a "Scott Schedule" nature. After applying these considerations there must remain a debatable boundary area between cases which clearly are official referees' business and those which clearly are not. What can be said is that if there is a considerable amount of detail to be investigated; if there are matters of account involved; if there are issues to be determined in the light of the expert evidence of engineers, architects or surveyors: these are official referees' business. But questions turning on the expert evidence of the medical profession are not. The boundary line may perhaps be illustrated by taking the instance of a sale of goods case. If the issue is whether the contract was made or what were its terms, it is not strictly official referees' business (although it can of course be referred if the parties agree). But if the issue is whether a quantity of goods corresponds with sample or exhibit defects, so that a number of individual articles have to be considered, or expert evidence has to be given, then it is official referees' business.

[1] Para. 1–05 above.
[2] Para. 4–04 above.
[3] Ord. 72, r.1(2). "In this Order 'commercial action' includes any cause arising out of the ordinary transactions of merchants and traders, and, without prejudice to the generality of the foregoing words, any cause relating to the construction of a mercantile document, the export or import of merchandise, affreightment, insurance, banking, mercantile agency and mercantile usage."

Where both sorts of issue arise in the same case, reference may well be ordered. In practice all building construction, engineering construction, and dilapdidations cases are prima facie official referees' business.

## Grounds for excluding cases

A litigant who wishes to transfer to the parent division a case started   **6–04**
in the official referees' court, or to resist an application to transfer a case to it, may assert either that it was not official referees' business or that, if prima facie it is official referees' business there are special reasons for assigning it to the ordinary lists of the Chancery or Queen's Bench Divisions. The special reasons exemplified in the reported cases are ordinarily the gravity of the matter coupled with the absence of a right of appeal on fact.

## Gravity of the case

In the early days of official referees' operations questions involving a   **6–05**
person's reputation were thought unfit for reference. In *Leigh* v. *Brooks*,[4] a case about the valuation of a picture, fraud was alleged against the defendant, who appealed against an order under section 57 of the 1873 Act referring the case. Jessel M.R. said[5]:

> "This case is one in which the fortune and character of Mr. Brooks are at stake, and what is asked is to deprive him of the advantage of having the case decided by a judge in a public court in the presence of the bar, and to oblige him to have it tried in a private room before a judge of inferior standing."

James L.J. added that a man was entitled to insist on an allegation of fraud being tried in open court. That was in 1877; for many decades now all official referee's trials have been held in open court. And as the old procedure of inquiry and report fell into disuse more and more cases of fraud or professional negligence came to be referred. However in 1932 section 1 of the Administration of Justice Act of that year radically altered appeals from official referees and in so doing abolished the right of appeal on matters of fact.[6] This introduced a new factor into the question whether or not to remit. The courts' attitude to this new factor was ultimately crystallised by the decision of the House of Lords in *Osenton & Co.* v. *Johnston*,[7] a case of alleged professional negligence by surveyors. The Master had ordered referral and had been upheld by the judge in chambers and by a majority of the Court of Appeal. But the

---

[4] (1877) 5 Ch.D. 592.
[5] *Ibid.* at 595.
[6] Para. 14–01 below.
[7] [1942] A.C. 130.

House of Lords found that the discretion to refer had been wrongly exercised, Viscount Simon L.C. approved the principle of *Leigh* v. *Brooks*[8] and said that although negligence fell far short of fraud nevertheless the objection that there was no appeal on fact ought to be given full weight.[9] Lord Simon also approved the dissenting judgment of Clauson L.J. in the Court of Appeal. In that judgment the nature of this objection to transfer was summarised as follows[10]:

> "The effect of the section [then section 1 of the Administration of Justice Act 1932, now Order 58, rule 5] is to put it out of the power of the judge to refer such a case as this without at the same time depriving the parties of the right of appeal in case of error of fact which they would have in the case of trial before a judge . . . The position of a judge who is asked to order a compulsory reference in a case to which this section applies is far more difficult than before the Act came into force."

In approving this approach Lord Simon added[11]:

> "In considering whether to transfer a case to the official referee where all the parties do not consent the Master or a judge must always have fully in mind and give due weight to the alternative of trial by judge alone."

### Professional negligence cases

6–06     In consequence of the decision in *Osenton & Co.* v. *Johnston* the law was altered and appeal on fact reintroduced in the case of professional negligence. Since then cases of negligence by architects, surveyors and engineers have been regularly tried as official referees' business. But there remain other cases where a party may wish to preserve a right of appeal on fact and where the court in its discretion thinks it just so to do. Such a case was *Simplicity Products Co.* v. *Domestic Installations Co. Ltd.*[12] This was a negligence case in which the Court of Appeal reversed the decision to transfer to the official referee. Lord Denning M.R. said[13]:

> "Here the question is as to the suitability of a product which was manufactured and supplied by the plaintiffs on a large scale. It affects their standing as a supply company. The issues are very proper to be tried by a judge alone and reviewed if need be by the Court of Appeal . . . Mr. Sheridan suggested certain advantages

---

[8] (1877) 5 Ch.D. 592.
[9] *Osenton & Co.* v. *Johnston* [1942] A.C. 130 at 138.
[10] *Johnston* v. *Osenton & Co* [1940] 2 K.B. 123 at 138.
[11] *Osenton & Co.* v. *Johnston* [1942] A.C. 130 at 135.
[12] [1973] 1 W.L.R. 837.
[13] *Ibid.* at 840.

before an official referee, such as that he himself holds the summons for directions, he has himself a control over the course of the proceedings; he can hold views and so forth. But those advantages do not outweigh the serious disadvantage of there being no appeal on fact. The questions here are of such importance to the parties that they should be tried by a judge alone."

On the other hand, if there is appeal on fact, as in the professional negligence cases, the gravity or importance of the matter is no ground for denying trial by official referee. See *Scarborough R.D.C.* v. *Moore*[14] where a local authority brought an action against a consulting engineer alleging negligence. The damages were estimated at £500,000. The district registrar ordered trial by High Court judge but on appeal Milmo J. ordered trial by official referee. The defendant appealed to the Court of Appeal who dismissed the appeal. Lord Denning M.R. noted that the decision of the House of Lords in *Osenton & Co.* v. *Johnston* was no longer applicable because of the alteration in the rules whereby the right of appeal was conferred on fact in professional negligence cases. As to remission, "each case had to be considered on its own circumstances. The council's estimate was that it would take three months to go into all the documents, and the formidable particulars which the court had seen would take many weeks to try. Was it really suitable for a High Court judge?"[15] The Master of the Rolls concluded that despite the fact that this was a charge of negligence against a professional man the case, because of its complexity and detail, was proper to be tried before an official referee.

Despite these authorities, such appeals are not to be encouraged. See *per* Lord Simon in *Osenton & Co.* v. *Johnston*[16]:

"It is most undesirable to limit, by unnecessary rulings, the reasonable ambit of the work which official referees undertake and discharge so greatly to the public benefit."

### Preserving appeal on fact

It sometimes happens that parties wish to preserve a right of appeal 6–07 on fact but also wish to avail themselves of the expertise in construction cases which the official referees are considered to possess. For this purpose it is possible to make use of the official referees' ability to sit, when so directed, as judges of the Queen's Bench Division. If the Clerk of the Lists agrees to list the case before an official referee sitting as a Queen's Bench judge, and the official referee agrees to this course, the desired result can be achieved. This procedure has been followed in one or two

[14] (1968) 112 S.J. 986.
[15] *Ibid.*
[16] [1942] A.C. 130 at 147.

cases since the Courts Act 1971 came into force, but there is no entitle-
ment to it and whether it can be arranged depends on the state of business in the Queen's Bench non-jury list and the official referees' lists.

### Jurisdiction in construction cases

6–08    In 1984 the Court of Appeal decided a case which has had a profound
effect upon the practice of the official referees' courts in construction
cases. This case, *Northern Regional Health Authority* v. *Crouch Construction Co. Ltd.*[17] arose out of contracts between a building owner (the
Health Authority), a main contractor (Crouch), and a sub-contractor
(Crown). The relevant contract was in the standard form, in use for
many years in the building industry. It contained, as do most building
contracts, an arbitration clause *inter alia* giving the arbitrator power:

> "to open up, review and revise any certificate, opinion, decision,
> requirement or notice and to determine all matters in dispute
> which shall be submitted to him in the same manner as if no such
> certificate, opinion, decision, requirement or notice had been
> given."

A series of disputes arose between the parties. Some were being submitted to arbitration; some were being litigated. The appeal arose out of
an attempt by the Health Authority to divert two of the disputes from
arbitration to litigation. They applied by originating summons to the
official referee for an injunction restraining Crouch and Crown from
seeking awards in two arbitrations. Judge Smout Q.C. dismissed the
applications, holding that on the facts injustice would be done if they
were acceded to. The Court of Appeal agreed with Judge Smout and
with his reasons, but they added a further reason which had not been
argued before him. They held that the official referees' court would not
have the powers which an arbitrator would have under the above-
mentioned words of the arbitration clause. This was a novel decision.
Hitherto the official referees had always, in their frequent dealings with
this type of case, assumed the powers conferred by the arbitration
clause.[18] The practice had been recorded in the following terms by
Judge Stabb Q.C.[19] in an earlier round in the same series of conflicts:

> "If the parties, as in this case, are able to choose the court as a
> forum for litigation rather than an arbitrator for arbitration, the

---

[17] [1984] Q.B. 644.
[18] See *Hudson on Building Contracts* (10th ed.), p. 832: *Keating on Building Contracts* (4th
ed.), p. 414. But note that this procedure had been doubted by Judge Newey Q.C. in
*Holland Hannen & Cubitts Ltd.* v. *Welsh Health Technical Services Organisation* (1981) 18
Build. L.R. 80 at 121.
[19] Following *Neale* v. *Richardson* [1938] 1 All E.R. 753 and *Prestige & Co. Ltd.* v. *Brettell*
[1938] 4 All E.R. 346.

court is invested with the same powers as the contract bestows upon the arbitrator and the court, after determining the issue, can give judgment for the payment of any money which that determination shows to be due."[20]

The Court of Appeal held that this view was wrong. Brown-Wilkinson L.J., after citing the powers conferred upon an arbitrator to open up or revise any architect's certificate etc., said:

"If in any litigation the official referee also has such power there is no problem. But if the official referee does not have such power any injunction restraining the continuation of the arbitration proceedings would deprive Crouch . . . of rights which they enjoy under the contract. So much is common ground.

What then are the powers of the official referee? It appears that there are two separate types of proceedings which may come before the official referee. First the parties may by an arbitration agreement appoint the official referee as arbitrator under section 11 of the Arbitration Act 1950. If this is done the official referee plainly has all the powers conferred upon the arbitrator by the agreement of the parties. We were told that such a procedure is nowadays very rare. Secondly (and this is the normal case such as the present) one of the parties having started ordinary High Court proceedings, the court may refer the matter to the official referee.[21] In such a case the powers of the official referee are regulated by R.S.C., Ord. 36, r. 4, which, in effect, confer on him all the powers of the court making the reference.

Accordingly, although the official referee's business is regarded as a special category of business and in practice official referees treat themselves as having jurisdiction to exercise all the powers conferred upon an arbitrator by the standard form of building contract, the official referee can in fact have no wider powers than a judge of the Queen's Bench Division if an action relating to the building contract were to be heard by him."[22]

The judge went on to hold that a judge of the Queen's Bench Division would not have power to open up, review or revise an architect's certificate, *ergo* the official referee had no such power. He said:

"As a matter of principle I reach the conclusion that if this matter were to be litigated in the High Court (whether before the official

---

[20] Unreported; cited by Donaldson M.R. in *Northern Regional Health Authority* v. *Crouch Construction Co. Ltd.* above.

[21] This passage ignores the direct procedure, introduced in 1982, whereby the writ is marked "official referees business" and there is no "reference" but *semble* the same reasoning would apply in such cases.

[22] *Northern Regional Health Authority* v. *Crouch Construction Ltd.* [1984] Q.B. 644 at 666–667.

referee or a judge) the court would not have power to open up review and revise certificates or opionions as it thought fit since so to do would be to modify the contractual obligations of the parties."[23]

Dunn L.J. and Donaldson M.R. gave judgments to the like effect.[24]

### Effect of the Crouch case

**6–09**    The decision in *Crouch* was received by those concerned with construction disputes with emotions varying from surprise to consternation. It is probably *obiter*, but it has been generally followed. It has been heavily, not to say bitterly, attacked[25] and there is a school of thought that holds that it need not be followed because it conflicts with previous decisions of the House of Lords. However, unless it is overruled it will be followed by the official referees[26] and it has been cited with approval by another Court of Appeal.[27] For the official referees' courts it has had several effects. First it has decisively rejected the view that the official referees had a wider jurisdiction than the High Court because of their arbitral origins, a matter referred to in paragraph 21–06 below. Other consequences were foreshadowed by Donaldson M.R. when at the conclusion of his judgment he said:

> "It may be that the indications which we have given that, in the absence of a written submission to arbitration [the official referees] do not have jurisdiction to exercise the powers of an arbitrator . . . will reduce the length of the lists. I say this because our view, if accepted, will virtually give any party a right of veto on any attempt to bypass the arbitration clauses . . . If this reduction in the length of the lists does not occur or seems unlikely to occur, urgent consideration should be given to conferring upon the official referees a power analogous to that contemplated by section 92 of the County Courts Act 1959 to enable the official referees, whether sitting as such or as arbitrators, to refer or sub-refer, the 'nuts and bolts' of the suit to a suitably qualified arbitrator for inquiry and report. This would result in the official referees becoming, in effect, the construction industry court, having the same relationship to the construction industry as the Commercial Court has to the financial and commercial activities of the City of London. It could decide

---

[23] *Ibid.* at 667.
[24] *Ibid.* at 663–664 and 670–673.
[25] *Cf.* "Construction Contracts: the Architect, the Arbitrator and the Courts" by I. N. Duncan Wallace Q.C., 2 Cons.L.J. 13.
[26] See *Oram Builders Ltd.* v. *M. J. Pemberton* (1985) Con.L.R. 94; 2 Cons.L.R. 94; *Douglas R. M. Construction Ltd.* v. *Welsh Health Technical Services Organisation & Others* (1985) 5 Con.L.R. 90.
[27] *Tubeworkers Ltd.* v. *Tilbury Construction Ltd.* (1985) 30 Build.L.R. 67.

questions of principle which are of general interest, leaving it to the individual arbitrators to apply those principles to the details of individual disputes."[28]

The reduction in the length of the lists, expected by the Master of the Rolls, has not come about,[29] although there are at present signs that the intake is levelling off. There has, however, undoubtedly been a reduction in building contract cases entering the lists because a large proportion of such disputes involve challenging an architect's decision,[30] and there has been a modest increase in the number of arbitrations submitted to the official referees under section 11 of the Arbitration Act 1950. Other changes adumbrated by the Master of the Rolls may lie in the future, although one has already been brought into force. This is the transfer from the Commercial Court to the official referees' court of appeals from arbitrators in construction cases, and applications for leave to appeal in such cases. As to this see paragraph 20–08 below.

---

[28] *Northern Regional Health Authority* v. *Crouch Construction Ltd.* [1984] Q.B. 644 at 674–675.
[29] See Table 1, Appendix F, para. F–01 below.
[30] However if the parties expressly agree they can perhaps confer arbitrator's powers on an official referee: *Partington & Son (Builders) Ltd.* v. *Tameside M.B.C.* (1985) 32 Build.L.R. 150; and see *Keating on Building Contracts* (4th ed.), p. 414.

47

# Chapter 7
# Initial Procedure

### Writ or originating summons

**7–01**   The direct procedure for commencing proceedings in the official referees' court, brought ino effect on October 1, 1982, is governed by rule 2(1) of Order 36, which runs as follows:

> "Before the issue of a writ or originating summons by which official referees' business is to be begun, it may be marked in the top left hand corner with the words 'official referees' business' and, on the issue of the writ or summons so marked, the cause or matter begun thereby shall be treated as official referees' business."

The writ or summons is issued in the normal way out of the London office or a district registry. It is left to the litigant to decide whether his case can properly be marked as official referees' business, the only restriction being that no cause or matter to which Her Majesty or the Duke of Cornwall is a party may be tried before an official referee without their consent.[1] But a litigant who starts in the official referees' court a case which is plainly not official referees' business faces the risk of having the case transferred to the Chancery or Queen's Bench Division, as the case may be, and of having to pay the costs of transfer. Where he is satisfied that his case can properly be marked "official referees' business" he has the option of so marking it or of leaving it unmarked, in which event it will either be dealt with according to the ordinary procedure of the parent division, or will be subsequently transferred to the official referees' court, as mentioned in the next paragraph.

### Service out of the jurisdiction

**7–02**   If a writ or originating summons marked "official referees' business" is intended to be served out of the jurisdiction the application for leave to do so under Order 11 rule 1 must be made to an official referee.[2] The

---

[1] Ord. 36, r. 12.
[2] Ord. 36, r. 2(2).

application is made by lodging the affidavit required by Order 11, rule 4 with the clerk to the senior official referee. The affidavit must state that the writ or originating summons is intended to be marked "official referees' business."[3] The official referee may indorse a decision on the affidavit or may require the applicant to attend a hearing. If the official referee hearing such an application is of opinion that the cause or matter should not be dealt with as official referees' business he may adjourn the application to be heard by a Master.[4]

### Transfer

Side by side with the direct procedure the old provisions as to transfer from the Queen's Bench or Chancery Divisions are continued. The transfer provisions are now contained in rule 3 of Order 36:

    "3(1) At any stage before the trial of a cause or matter in the Chancery Division or Queen's Bench Division any party may apply by summons to the Court to transfer the proceedings to be dealt with as official referees' business."

7–03

Transfer is employed in cases where the parties wish to have the case heard as official referees' business but from inadvertence or otherwise the writ was not so marked in the first instance, or in cases where it is the defendant who takes the initiative in having the case transferred to the official referees' court. Transfer may be applied for on an ad hoc summons before the Master (or District Registrar), and if granted the transfer order will be made in form PF74, ordering that "the whole of this cause be transferred to an official referee and that the costs of the same be in the discretion of the official referee."[5] The rule provides that the application to transfer may be made at any stage before trial. In the past transfer orders, where not made on an early ad hoc summons, have not infrequently been made on a Master's summons for directions or in Order 14 proceedings or even later. If however the case is to be transferred the earlier it is done the better, because of the control which the official referees expect to exercise over the whole of the interlocutory stages of the action.[6]

### Transfer by the court

An express power introduced by the 1982 rules is the power of the court to transfer of its own motion. By Order 36, rule 3(2):

7–04

    "If the Court considers that any cause or matter in the Chancery

---

[3] Ord. 36, r. 2(3).
[4] Ord. 36, r. 2(4).
[5] See *The Supreme Court Practice 1988*, Vol. 2, para. 278.
[6] See para. 7–06 below.

Division or Queen's Bench Division may more appropriately be dealt with as official referees' business, the Court may of its own motion, but subject to any right to a trial with a jury, order that the cause or matter, or any question or issue of fact arising therein, shall be tried by an official referee."

This power probably existed previously in the inherent right of the court to control its procedure but it was rarely used. Occasionally a judge, confronted with a case which ought clearly to be official referees' business, has refused to try it and has transferred it, but this is frowned upon.[7] However, whether transfer is made of the court's own motion before trial or after trial, the parties are entitled to be consulted:

"3(4) No order for the transfer of proceedings shall be made by the court or an official referee under this rule unless the parties have either—
(a) had an opportunity of being heard on the issue, or
(b) consented to such an order."

A similar power to transfer in the other direction is now also given to an official referee if he considers that the cause or matter "may more appropriately be tried by a Master or judge." He may do this of his own motion or on the application of any party.[8]

### Transfer of issues

7–05    Under the rules as they existed before October 1982 the court could transfer "the cause or matter or any question or issue of fact arising therein" to the official referees. It is to be observed that under the new rules the right of the parties to apply for transfer is limited to transfer of "the proceedings," *i.e.* the whole case. However the power to transfer a question or issue of fact remains in paragraph (2) of rule 3 as a power exercisable by the court of its own motion. In the past issues have often been transferred where it seemed convenient or advantageous so to do, sometimes before trial of the remainder of the case and sometimes by the trial court after trial—or by the Court of Appeal. Issue transfer after trial is especially appropriate to deciding the quantum of damages and is an alternative to the assessment of damages by an official referee after a judgment has been signed.[9] The new structure of the rules appears to put the emphasis as regards issue transfer on the class of case where the court, having decided part of the case, decides to remit another part; but presumably a party, although denied the right to apply by summons for

---

[7] *cf. Ullstrom* v. *Naar* [1939] 1 K.B. 697, where Lord Hewart C.J. referred a case after hearing the opening; the Court of Appeal disapproved.
[8] Ord. 36, r. 3(3).
[9] See Chap. 18 below.

transfer of an issue, could raise the matter upon another summons, for example a summons for directions, and ask the Master or Registrar to act "of his own motion," especially if the parties were agreed upon this course. Partial transfer would appear to be especially advisable in Admiralty cases if it is desired to retain in the Admiralty court that court's peculiar powers in actions *in rem.*

### Effect of treatment as official referees' business

Where under rule 2(1) a writ or originating summons is marked "official referees' business" and where under rule 3(1) a case is ordered to be transferred, the proceedings are "to be dealt with as official referees' business." This means that they are removed, in the first case from the outset and in the second case from the date of the order, from the control of the parent division and that the official referee alone has power to hear and determine interlocutory applications. To this proposition there is one statutory exception, made for convenience. This exception is that by Order 64, rule 6(2) a Master or District Registrar may hear applications for interlocutory orders during the Long Vacation. This was a useful provision for dealing with urgent matters at a time when no official referee was available. But with the increased business of recent years the official referees have begun sitting on some days in the vacations, including the Long Vacation. The present practice as regards summonses is that an official referee is available during all vacations. Inquiries about urgent matters should be made at the office (open in the Long Vacation from 10 a.m. to 2.30 p.m.) and there is now no reason for taking out a Master's summons in the Long Vacation. The exception does not apply to the other vacations. With this exception, transfer of the whole case extinguishes the Master's jurisdiction, and when, as sometimes happens through inadvertence or ignorance of procedure, an order is made by a Master who is not told that the case has been transferred, the order is a nullity. The position in this regard was explored in full in *Durston* v. *O'Keefe.*[10] In that case a district registrar had transferred the action but nevertheless directed that all interlocutory applications should come before him, the district registrar. Forbes J. held that this could not be done. He said[11]:

7–06

> "Once the District Registrar has made an order referring the cause as official referees' business there is nothing further for him to do. The circuit judge then becomes seized of the matter and under rule 6 the cause must be entered with that circuit judge's clerk. . . . Any application for directions must then be made in accordance with rule 6, to the circuit judge to whom the cause has been allocated."

[10] [1974] 1 W.L.R. 777.
[11] *Ibid.* at 778.

Forbes J. went on to explain that there was good reason for this course[12]:

> "One of the great advantages of the procedure adopted in cases designated as official referees' business is that, as in the Commercial Court cases, the judge who will try the case has charge of it from the momemt of transfer. In dealing with the interlocutory matters he is able to propose the procedures to be adopted and the steps to be followed to meet the needs of each case with a view to minimising costs in a class of litigation which, by virtue of its complexity, is potentially expensive."[13]

In *Durston* v. *O'Keefe* it had been argued that the District Registrar had been empowered to make the order which he did by virtue of Order 32, rule 11, which authorises Masters (and District Registrars) to transact "all such business as under the Act [the Supreme Court of Judicature (Consolidation) Act 1925[14]] or these rules may be transacted by a judge in chambers"; but:

> " 'Those words must mean a High Court judge in chambers, but Order 36, rule 6 is not dealing with the transaction of business by a High Court judge in chambers, it is dealing with the transaction of business by a circuit judge discharging the functions of an official referee.' Accordingly in my judgment the point has no validity and Order 32, rule 11 does not apply to the discharge of business by those circuit judges."[15]

In *Durston* v. *O'Keefe* it was also submitted that the making of orders by a District Registrar after transfer to an official referee was a mere irregularity which under Order 2, rule 1 could be treated as not nullifying the orders. Forbes J. rejected this argument also, saying: "Mr. Brodie contends that this is not a mere irregularity but a question of want of jurisdiction and I consider that he is right."[16] The District Registrar's orders were accordingly set aside as having been made without jurisdiction.

The decision in *Durston* v. *O'Keefe* was upon the effect of a transfer order but its reasoning must apply equally to a case started in the official referees' court—a proposition recognised by the special pro-

---

[12] *Ibid.* at 779.
[13] See also Sir Francis Newbolt, "Expedition and Economy in Litigation," (1923) 39 L.Q.R. 427 at 437: "There is no greater check on wasteful expenditure than the arrangement by which the trial judge takes his own summonses, especially if he makes notes of them upon the file."
[14] Now the Supreme Court Act 1981.
[15] [1974] 1 W.L.R. 777 at 780.
[16] *Ibid.*

vision made for the official referees to deal with applications for leave to serve an official referees' business writ outside the jurisdiction.[17]

### Effect of partial transfer

The law as set out in the last preceding paragraph has no application to instances where only part of a case is transferred. If defined issues only are referred for trial by an official referee the rest of the case remains with the parent division and is subject to that division's directions. It is advisable to employ partial transfer in admiralty cases if it is desired to retain in the Admiralty Court that court's peculiar powers in actions *in rem*.

**7–07**

### The rota system[18]

The new rules require an application for directions to be made to "the official referee to whom the business has been allocated." The allocation is by rota. By Order 36, rule 5(1):

**7–08**

> "No writ or originating summons by which official referees' business is to be begun and no order referring any business to an official referee under these rules shall specify any particular referee."

And by rule 5(3):

> "Official referees' business in the Royal Courts of Justice shall be allocated by the rota clerk to the official referees in rotation."

Allocation of the judge by rota was not always the case. Originally the parties could choose their referee; subsequently a rota system was introduced for cases where the parties had no preference. Finally in 1957 the rule in its present form was adopted. The original option to the parties to choose their judge was another aspect of official referee's work derived from the procedure in arbitration, but in practice it led to inequalities in the work load of the official referees, and the present rule has the effect, *inter alia*, of equalising their lists.[19]

### Office procedure

As a first step after receiving notice of intention to defend, or after the transfer order, as the case may be, a party or his solicitor should have his case rota'd in the official referees' office. Normally it is the plaintiff who takes this step, but there is no reason why the defendant should

**7–09**

---

[17] Para. 6–08, above.
[18] Paras. 7–08 to 7–11 deal with the practice in London, including the South-Eastern Circuit: for the different practice in the provinces, see Chap. 15 below.
[19] See para. 4–04 above.

not enter the case if the plaintiff fails to act. The procedure in the office is no longer the subject of a rule[20] but the administrative arrangements are as follows. The original writ or originating summons and (if it is a transferred case) the original transfer order, together with a copy of each document, should be taken to the office of the rota clerk. He will enter the case on the rota and will retain the copy documents for the file and return the originals marked with the name of the official referee assigned.[21] The rota clerk then opens a file for the case and passes the file to the clerk to the assigned judge. The case now takes its place in that judge's list. The party who has rota'd the case should give notice of the fact to the other party or parties to the cause or matter or to their solicitors. Ordinarily a summons for directions is taken out at the same time.

### Fees

7–10    Entry on the rota is taken to be the equivalent of setting down, and accordingly the setting down fee, at present £30, must be paid. Either a praecipe on Form E26 should be stamped or the filed copy of the pleadings is receipted and the receipt must be produced to the rota clerk. The fee is provided for in item B5 of section 1 of the Schedule to the Supreme Court Fees Order 1980: "on fixing a date for the trial of a cause or matter before an official referee: £30."[22] The requirement is subject to exceptions preventing double payment, including exception (c): "where, in the case of a reference to an official referee the fee has already been paid in respect of the same cause or matter." Thus only one fee need be paid although there may be two trials as for instance a trial between a plaintiff and a defendant followed by a trial between a defendant and a third party. However a further fee of £15 is payable on each summons for directions.

### The rota book

7–11    The rota clerk keeps a rota book in which all incoming references are entered. The requirement of Order 36, rule 5(3) that business shall be allocated to the referees in rotation is strictly observed. Its importance was emphasised by the Court of Appeal in the case of *Shrager* v. *Basil Dighton Ltd.*[23] In that case the rota clerk had been prevailed upon to allocate a case to the senior official referee, who could hear it speedily, instead of the next referee upon the rota, who was engaged on a long

---

[20] Until October 1982 it was a specific requirement of Ord. 36, r. 5(3) that the transfer order be produced to the clerk to the Senior Official Referee.

[21] See the Procedure Notice, Appendix C below.

[22] Supreme Court Fees Order 1980 (S.I. 1980 No. 821); *The Supreme Court Practice 1988*, Vol. 2, para. 1004.

[23] [1924] 1 K.B. 274.

case, or the next but one, who was unwell. The senior official referee had agreed to this course being taken. Bankes L.J. said:

> "It has been suggested that under these rules some discretion as to the allocation of business is vested in the clerk to the senior official referee or in the senior official referee himself. I do not agree with this suggestion. It is in my opinion clear that the duty of the clerk is mechanical merely and that the senior official referee has no authority at all to interfere with that mechanical duty. No doubt a strict interpretation of the rules may sometimes result in difficulties and inconveniences. The remedy is to improve the rules and is not to be found in disregarding them."[24]

The Divisional Court and the majority of the Court of Appeal found that the clerk's action in this case was a bona fide mistake; Atkin L.J. however was more censorious, terming the matter "a grave impropriety."[25]

### Hearing by another referee

Difficulties of the kind exemplified in *Shrager* v. *Basil Dighton Ltd.* are **7–12** unlikely to arise today because, following a recommendation of the Evershed Committee[26] it is now possible to transfer a case from one official referee to another: Order 36, rule 7(2): "Any official referee may order the transfer of any business from himself to any other official referee who consents to the transfer." There is sometimes a good practical reason for a case to be assigned to a particular referee; conversely there may be a good reason for an individual referee not to take a case. The former situation arises in practice where one referee is already seized of a case having some relationship with the new case. If the suits are obviously destined for consolidation or for trial one with the other or if the new action is so related in subject-matter with the existing case that time will be saved by the same judge trying both, then the relevant facts should be mentioned to the rota clerk and, provided both parties agree, he will be able to secure transfer to the judge who has the existing case in his list, if the chance of the rota has not already alighted upon that judge.[27] Typical examples of such a situation are where successive writs are issued claiming successive instalments of remuneration due under a building contract, or where the first case is litigation between building owner and main contractor and the second case is a dispute between that main contractor and a sub-contractor in the same work. An example where transfer from, rather than to, an official referee

---

[24] *Ibid.* at 281.
[25] The Court of Appeal held however that by proceeding with knowledge of the facts the appellants had waived the irregularity.
[26] See para. 4–04 above.
[27] This is effected by transfer under Ord. 36, r. 7(2), see para. 15–05 below.

would arise would be where the official referee next in rotation was acquainted with one of the parties to the litigation. For transfer of applications for directions, see paragraph 8–09 below.

### Procedure in the provinces

7–13    Different provisions apply to cases proceeding in district registries other than those on the south eastern circuit. In cases assigned to provincial referees the taking out of the summons for directions is the equivalent of entering upon the rota.

# Chapter 8
# Summons for Directions

## The rules

Under R.S.C., Order 36, rule 6(1) it is the duty of the plaintiff to apply **8–01** for directions within 14 days of the giving by the defendant of a notice of intention to defend, or the date of the order transferring the cause or matter. Rule 6(2) provides that if the plaintiff does not so apply any other interested party may apply to strike out pleadings or to dismiss the claim or the counterclaim as the case may be. If another party makes an application under sub-rule (2) the official referee may accede to it or may deal with the matter as an application for directions: Order 36, rule 6(3).[1]

This requirement for an early summons ordinarily before pleadings, contrasts with the ordinary procedure where by Order 25, rule 1(1) the summons for directions is to be taken out within one month after close of pleadings. It is a special characteristic of official referees' business that the judge considers the case at an early stage and takes charge of the directions: see the words of Forbes J. cited at paragraph 7–06 above.

## The practice

The application is made by summons, stamped £15. If it is a transfer **8–02** case and there was a summons for directions before the Master and when the case was transferred the Master adjourned this summons, it may be restored for hearing before the official referee. Otherwise the party applying must produce a draft summons to the rota clerk who will issue it and assign a hearing date. This is ordinarily done at the same time as entering the case upon the rota. The draft summons should be endorsed with an estimate of the length of the hearing and a statement

---

[1] For the full text of the rule see Appendix B, below, para. B–09.

as to whether or not it is with counsel.[2] Short summonses (less than 15 minutes) are heard by the judge before 10.30 a.m. on the assigned date: long summonses (15 minutes or over) are heard on Fridays. They are heard "in court as chambers." The 14-day rule is honoured rather more in the breach than in the observance, but undue delay in seeking the first order for directions is disadvantageous to a plaintiff in that it post-pones *pro tanto* the date for the hearing of his claim. Parties ordinarily attend by solicitors or counsel, but they may be heard in person. If an officer of a limited company desires to appear on behalf of his company he should apply to the judge at the hearing and he may be accorded audience if there is some good reason why the company cannot instruct a solicitor.

### The form

8–03    The rules do not require particularity in the summons for directions. By Order 36, rule 6(4) the provisions of Order 25, rules 2 to 7 are made applicable to official referees' proceedings. Order 25 is the order provid-ing for directions generally in Queen's Bench and Chancery Division proceedings, but it is applied with the omission of any requirement to specify the orders sought. Thus Order 25, rule 1 is omitted, and it is under this rule that the usual Master's summons for directions in Form PF51 is provided; furthermore, the application of Order 25, rule 7(1) is expressly stated to be "with the omission of so much of rule 7(1) as requires parties to serve a notice specifying the orders and directions which they desire."[3] For this reason the form in general use merely asks for "such directions as may be appropriate," or for "general directions." However parties not infrequently use fuller forms, either setting out in terms what they seek, or adapting Form PF51 by striking out irrelevant clauses, and this practice has the advantage of drawing any unusual features to the attention of the judge, with attendant saving of time and trouble.

### Pleadings to be lodged

8–04    Paragraph 1 of the Official Referees' Practice Direction of 1968,[4] requires all extant pleadings including further and better particulars to be lodged at the time of the issue of the first summons for directions. This can have no application to the direct procedure whereby the case is started as official referees' business because the summons for directions

---

[2] See the Procedure Notice issued by the Official Referees' Department, Appendix C below, para. C–02.

[3] See Appendix B, below, para B–09.

[4] [1968] 1 W.L.R. 425 and see Appendix C, below, para C–02.

ought to have been taken out before pleadings, but in transfer cases it must be followed. The Direction reflects the practice of the official referees to acquaint themselves with the nature of the case before the hearing of the summons. The official referees' clerk will have opened a file upon entry of the cause or matter, and in transfer cases the judge will expect to find upon it not only the basic court documents, *i.e.* the writ, the order of remission, and the summons for directions, but also the pleadings to date and any other relevant *inter partes* documents. Although the practice direction does not mention them, it is advantageous also to lodge copies of any affidavits hitherto used in Order 14 proceedings in the case and any orders made by the Master or District Registrar before the case was referred. The parties may assume when they arrive for the hearing of the summons for directions that the judge has read whatever papers have been lodged and is thus familiar with the general nature of the case. In cases started in the official referees' court they must be prepared to say what the issues are going to be.[5]

### Order 14 proceedings

In cases started as official referees' business all interlocutory applications must be made to the assigned judge and this includes Order 14 applications. The official referees' procedure has some attraction for plaintiffs because the hearing is by the judge, with appeal to the Court of Appeal, and the stage of appeal from Master to judge in chambers is omitted. Prior to the introduction of the new direct procedure in October 1982 the practice had grown up of Order 14 proceedings in building cases and the like being adjourned by the Master and the case including the Order 14 summons being transferred to the official referees. When this has been done the summons should be reinstated by application to the assigned official referee's clerk in lieu of taking out a summons for directions. In direct procedure cases the Order 14 summons is issued by the assigned official referees' clerk and must be supported by affidavit in the usual way. The clerk will require to be given an estimate of the time the hearing is anticipated to take. To avoid adjournments the official referee may order that no affadavit evidence be used on such a hearing save those of which copies have been served on the other party by a specified date. The hearing will be similar to the hearing of such a summons before the Master save that appeal will be to the Court of Appeal instead of to the judge in chambers. If the official referee gives leave to defend either conditionally or unconditionally he will consider whether to order that the affidavits stand as the pleadings

**8–05**

---

[5] See para. 8–06 below.

in the case and will give other directions as upon the first summons for directions.

### The hearing

8–06    The Practice Direction of 1968 states that "at the first summons for directions the solicitors should be in a position to state the nature of the claim and defence."[6] The first hearing has some of the characteristics of the preliminary meeting in an arbitration; the judge expects to be able to form some appreciation of the shape and nature of the contest so that he can devise a realistic programme of interlocutory events leading up to the trial. Part of the practice direction states that "At the hearing of the first summons before him, the official referee will give the necessary directions and make the necessary orders regarding the steps in the action to be taken by the parties."[7] The official referee will want to consider whether the case calls for a Scott Schedule,[8] whether preliminary issues should be singled out and tried separately,[9] and whether further parties are likely to be joined by way of amendment or third party proceedings. At the first summons it is to be expected that he will deal with pleadings, in a suitable case ordering trial without pleadings or ordering that the Order 14 affidavits stand as pleadings, and in the ordinary case ordering any further pleadings or particulars that are needed. He may also be expected at this stage to order a Scott Schedule if the case calls for it, and to provide for discovery by way of lists of documents and subsequent inspection of documents. Discovery may of course proceed under the rules without any order but the official referees prefer to make express orders in order to fit discovery into their timetable. In a simple case, the judge will be able to go on to give the remaining directions, usual among them being directions as to expert witnesses[10] and date and place of trial.[11] As to date of trial however it is to be noted that when Order 36, rule 6 was amended in October 1982 it introduced a specific requirement that the application for directions should include an application for a fixed date for hearing[12] and that this is intended to emphasise the need for an early fixing of the date. In many cases however the summons will be adjourned so that expert evidence and date and length of trial can be considered in the light of such further events as the completion of the Scott Schedule, the inspection of the disclosed documents, or the bringing in of further parties and the closing of their pleadings.

[6] See Appendix C, below, para. C–01.
[7] *Ibid.*
[8] See Chap. 9 below.
[9] See para. 12–09 below.
[10] See para. 9–03 below.
[11] See para. 13–04 below.
[12] For full text of the rule see Appendix B, below, para. B–09.

## Adjourned summons for directions

If some directions are left over because the case is not yet ready for **8–07** them the practice is to adjourn the summons to a fixed date by which time it is etimated that the further steps to be taken will permit of the rest of the directions being given. The alternative method of adjourning generally with liberty to the parties to apply may be adopted, but the official referees prefer the fixed date as more likely to secure progress. In large and complicated cases the device is sometimes employed of eventually adjourning the summons for directions to a date several weeks before the date fixed for the trial to commence, so that the parties can be required to reassemble for a pre-trial conference.[13] And in these cases the official referees encourage plaintiffs' counsel to circulate before the hearing a written summary of their opening speeches.

## Official referees' powers as to directions

By Order 36, rule 4(1)(a) an official referee has the same jurisdiction **8–08** powers and duties as a High Court judge for the purpose of disposing of any cause or matter "including any interlocutory application therein."[14] Any application for interlocutory relief which could be made to a Master or judge may be made to the Official Referee and may be asked for either on a summons for directions or upon an ad hoc summons. In almost all cases the judge will give directions as to pleadings, discovery of documents, the evidence of expert witnesses and date and place of trial. Other directions not infrequently met with in practice are further discovery verified by affidavit, security for costs, appointment of a court expert, the inspection and/or preservation of property, and the administration of interrogatories. It must be borne in mind that once a case is transferred to the official referee for trial all applications must be made to the official referee and a Master no longer has any jurisdiction to entertain such applications.[15] This matter needs emphasising as regards such applications as those under Order 67, rule 6 by a solicitor wishing to have his name taken off the record.

## Transfer to another official referee

Occasionally the subject-matter of an interlocutory application is **8–09** such that it is undesirable or improper for the assigned official referee to become aware of it. He it is who will try the case and some information relevant to the hearing of the summons may have to be withheld from the trial judge. A situation of this kind arises where a payment into

---

[13] See below, para. 12–09.
[14] See Appendix B, below, para. B–07.
[15] See para. 7–06 above.

court has to be mentioned.[16] It may be necessary to communicate the fact of payment into court to a judge on an interlocutory application.[17] This happens for example where security for costs is applied for and the amount of any payment in becomes relevant.[18]

This situation also arises where an application is made for an order requiring a defendant to make an interim payment under Order 29, Part II of the Rules of the Supreme Court.[19] Applications for such payments have not infrequently been made in the official referees' courts since the coming into force in 1980 of the new rules as to interim payments. In these and similar circumstances the applicant should mention the matter to the clerk when taking out his summons and arrangements will be made for the hearing of the application by another official referee, use being made of the machinery of transfer provided by Order 36, rule 7(3) which provides that any interlocutory application may be made to any other official referee, with his consent, and that that other official referee may deal with the application and make any order thereon which could have been made by the assigned official referee. After the relevant hearing the case will revert to the list of the official referee originally seized of it. A summons for direction may also occasionally be transferred to be heard by another official referee under Order 36, rule 7(3) for other reasons, such as the absence out of town or the illness of the assigned official referee. Sometimes, too, pressure of work leads an official referee to sit at an early hour on a part-heard case, in which event his short summons list will be transferred to and heard by a colleague.

### Order in party's absence

8–10   If upon the hearing of a summons for directions the applicant is represented but the respondent does not appear the official referee may make an order notwithstanding the respondent's absence. He will first

---

[16] " . . . no communication of that fact shall be made to the court at the trial or hearing of the action or counterclaim or of any question or issue as to the debt or damages until all questions of liability and of the amount of debt or damages have been decided." (Ord. 22, r. 7).

[17] *Williams* v. *Boag* [1941] 1 K.B. 1.

[18] See *Sir Lindsay Parkinson & Co. Ltd.* v. *Triplan Ltd.* [1973] 1 Q.B. 609, where the Court of Appeal held that under s.447 of the Companies Act 1948, the Court had a discretion whether or not to order security, especially *per* Lord Denning M.R. at 626: "The Court has a discretion which it will exercise considering all the circumstances of a particular case. . . . If there was a payment into court of a substantial sum of money (not merely a payment into court to get rid of a nuisance claim) that too would count."

[19] See Ord. 29, r. 15: "The fact that an order has been made under rule 11 or 12 shall not be pleaded and, unless the defendant consents or the Court so directs, no communication of that fact or of the fact that an interim payment has been made whether voluntarily or pursuant to an order shall be made to the court at the trial or hearing of any question or issue as to liability or damages until all questions of liability and amount have been determined."

have to be satisfied that the summons was served; ordinarily proof of service is accepted if a letter can be produced acknowledging service or even if the applicant's solicitor can state that he has been informed by the other side by telephone that it has been served. Failing such information the order will not be passed until an affidavit of service is brought in. Not infrequently the parties are able to agree beforehand upon the directions to be given and if this is the case it is sufficient for one party to attend and to produce a letter from the other party's solicitor specifying the agreed terms. Where there is no agreement and the respondent does not appear upon the first summons for directions the official referee is unlikely to make a controversial order or one dealing with later interlocutory stages or fixing a trial date. It is otherwise with later applications.

### Drawing up the order

At the conclusion of the hearing of the summons the judge's clerk will **8–11** endorse the directions made upon the summons and the judge will initial the endorsement. The applicant should next draw up a draft order in duplicate and take it to the judge's clerk, who will peruse and pass it.[20] Early service on other parties is essential if they were not present at the hearing.

### Summons for directions in Long Vacation

Although the Master ceases to have jurisdiction over cases wholly **8–12** remitted to an official referee[21] it is provided by Order 64, rule 6 that interlocutory orders or directions required in connection with a cause or matter pending before an official referee may in the Long Vacation be made or given by a Master of the Queen's Bench Division. This procedure would however seem to be obsolescent since official referees are now available to hear summonses in vacation.[22]

---

[20] Para. 3 of the Procedure Notice issued by the Official Referees' Department, Appendix C, below, para. C–02.
[21] *Durston* v. *O'Keefe* [1974] 1 W.L.R. 775, and see para. 7–06 above.
[22] See para. 7–06 above.

# Chapter 9
# Expert Evidence

## A court for experts

**9–01**    The great majority of official referees' cases involve the giving of expert evidence.[1] In the construction industry cases which form the bulk of the work the evidence of architects, building surveyors, quantity surveyors and structural engineers is commonplace. In other cases civil and mechanical engineers, scientists and experts from many fields of technology are called on to give evidence. Frequently the resolution of the dispute turns wholly or partly upon the court's view of the conflicting evidence of such expert witnesses. It has for many decades been the practice of the official referees' courts to require parties calling such witnesses to disclose their experts' reports well before the hearing so as to avoid surprise and to facilitate the understanding by counsel and the judge of the effect of the evidence and the points of disagreement. This practice was made of general application in the High Court by the introduction in 1974 of Part IV of Order 38 of the Rules of the Supreme Court, and it is those rules which form the framework within which the official referees' courts now deal with expert evidence.[2]

## The rules

**9–02**    By Order 38, rule 36(1) no expert evidence may be adduced at the trial or hearing unless (i) all parties agree, or (ii) the leave of the court has been obtained, or (iii) an application had been made to the court for a direction and any direction so given has been complied with. By Order 38, rule 38 on such an application as mentioned at (iii) above the court may, if satisfied that it is desirable to do so direct that the substance of any expert evidence which is to be adduced by any party be disclosed in

---

[1] "Expert evidence" is not limited to independent experts: it includes in-house experts and when giving such evidence, the parties themselves: *Shell Pensions Trust Ltd.* v. *Pell Frischmann & Partners* [1986] 2 All E.R. 911 (Judge Newey Q.C.).

[2] Para. 5 of the Official Referees' Practice Directions (Appendix C below) became obsolete upon the introduction of Part IV of Order 38, and should not now be followed.

the form of a written report or reports to such other parties and within such period as the court may specify. And in deciding whether to give such a direction the court must have regard to all the circumstances and may, to such extent as it thinks fit, treat any of the following circumstances as affording a sufficient reason for not giving such a direction: "(a) that the expert evidence is or will be based to any material extent upon a version of the facts in dispute between the parties; or (b) that the expert evidence is or will be based to any material extent upon facts which are neither (i) ascertainable by the expert by the exercise of his own powers of observation, nor (ii) within his general professional knowledge and experience."[3] The court is also empowered by Order 38, rule 4 to limit the number of expert witnesses. For expert evidence contained in a written statement see Order 38, rule 41. By Order 38, rule 38(3) the official referee now has power to order experts to meet without prejudice "for the purpose of identifying those parts of their evidence which are in issue." The experts may then prepare a joint statement indicating those parts of the evidence on which they are, and those in which they are not, in agreement.[3a]

## The practice

In a case requiring expert evidence it is customary on the hearing of    9–03
the summons for directions to ask for leave to call expert witnesses. This need not be expressly set out in the summons for directions[4] and if not mentioned at the hearing the official referee may himself raise the question. The raising of the matter is taken to be an application satisfying the requirements of Order 38, rule 36. The official referee will in an appropriate case give leave to call expert witnesses, but he will invariably couple with the leave a requirement that the written report of any witness to be called must be furnished to the other party or parties by a specified date. The order may take the form of a direction as mentioned in Ord. 36, r.38(1), or it may take the older form of making the giving of the leave conditional upon the furnishing of such reports. The official referee will also consider the question of limiting the number of experts to be called and in the smaller cases he may be expected to do so in order to limit costs incurred. In suitable cases he may require that experts in the same field meet without prejudice to try to narrow issues and agree figures by a date prior to delivery of reports. This practice, pioneered by the official referees, is now embodied in the compulsory

[3] Ord. 38, r.38(2).
[3a] As regards meetings of experts and exchange of statements of factual witnesses, reference may usefully be made to paras. XI and XII of the Guide to Commercial Court Practice set out in Appendix A to Ord. 72, *The Supreme Court Practice 1988*, p. 1109.
[4] See para. 8–03 above.

powers conferred by the new rule 38(3) of Order 38.[5] The date by which reports have to be furnished is ordinarily calculated with the trial date in mind in order that ample notice is given before the parties prepare for trial, but there are cases where an earlier disclosure of the respective technical cases facilitates the narrowing or settling of the issues, and in such cases earlier disclosure may be ordered. Otherwise the order will require disclosure so many months before the trial date, or by a date fixed with reference to the trial date. Sometimes parties speak of the "exchange" of experts' reports, but exchange as such is not necessary, and if one party complies with the direction or condition and the other party does not the one may call his experts and the other may not.

### Further orders

9–04    The experts may not strictly go outside the contents of their written reports. It sometimes happens that an expert wishes to reply to his adversary's report and in such cases application for leave ought to be made by summons in ample time before the hearing. Solicitors sometimes find that their experts are busy and unable to draft their report in time; in these cases a time summons ought to be taken out. The court may look indulgently on a few days extension of time but may be less amenable if the trial date is approaching. The judges like to look at the reports for themselves before the trial starts, and although there is usually no requirement as to service on the court it is in a party's interest to deliver a copy of any report to the judge's clerk at the same time as serving the other side.[6]

### Joint inspection

9–05    In some cases it is found to be useful to have a joint inspection of premises or plant, the subject-matter of an action, by the experts from both sides. This not infrequently happens in dilapidations cases and cases of allegedly defective building works. The parties' solicitors may be able to arrange such a joint inspection informally, but the court will in an appropriate case be able to assist by making an order under Order 29, rule 2(1) and (2) providing that named persons may enter upon the relevant property at a specified date and time for inspection purposes. Alternatively such a joint inspection may, formally or informally, be had at the same time as a view.[7] In the Scott Schedule type of case a joint inspection by surveyors has been found useful in promoting agreement upon some items and thus reducing the ambit of dispute.

[5] See para. 9–02 above.
[6] As to the "dossier" see para. 8–04 above.
[7] For views by the court, see para. 11–04 below.

## Default: sanctions

If default is made in complying with a condition or direction that an **9–06** expert's report be disclosed to other parties by a certain date, the effective sanction is that the defaulting party no longer has leave to call his expert evidence. This results from the wording of Order 38, rule 36(1): "no expert evidence may be adduced . . . unless the party has complied . . . with any directions given. . . . " The other party need take no steps to enforce the order; the sanction is automatic. A litigant who finds himself in default may only retrieve his expert evidence if his opponent agrees or if the judge thinks fit to give him leave notwithstanding his default. The latter course may involve an adjournment of the trial with costs falling on the defaulter.[8]

## Contents of the report

Each expert has his own style of reporting, but broadly speaking a **9–07** report should fall into two parts, firstly a description of the subject-matter and secondly the opinion of the expert upon the facts postulated. A good deal of technical language is inevitable, but the writer should bear in mind the fact this his report must be understood by counsel and the judge as well as by his colleagues on the other side. An official referee may be expected to be familiar with terms ordinarily used in building and engineering construction, but if more unusual or recondite matters are involved it may be useful to append a glossary. It has been judicially observed that the object of Part IV of Order 38 is "to save expense by dispensing with the calling of experts when there is in reality no dispute and, when there is a dispute, by avoiding parties being taken by surprise as to the true nature of the dispute and thereby being obliged to seek adjournments."[9]

## Joint independent experts

It was at one time the practice of the official referees in a suitable case **9–08** to pursuade the parties to agree to retain an independent expert jointly. From articles contributed by Sir Francis Newbolt (official referee 1920–36) to the *Law Quarterly Review* in 1923 and 1926[10] it is clear that at that time very many of the official referees' cases were dealt with in this way. The independent expert was jointly appointed and jointly paid by the parties and his report usually concluded the dispute. If not, he could

---

[8] See *Cable* v. *Dallaturca* (1977) 121 S.J. 795 (a road accident case) where Cantley J. gave late leave but awarded the successful plaintiff only half of his costs of the trial "in order to mark the view which the court took of the importance of the rule."

[9] *Per* Ackner J. in *Ollett* v. *Bristol Aerojet Ltd.* [1979] 1 W.L.R. 1197.

[10] "Expedition and Economy in Litigation," (1923) 39 L.Q.R. 427; "Avoidable Waste," (1926) 42 L.Q.R. 52.

be cross-examined by both sides. It is not known when the practice fell into desuetude but it has not been employed within the memory of those now connected with the court. Perhaps it lost vitality when formalised in the Rules of the Supreme Court, as mentioned in the next paragraph. Perhaps it should be revived. Sir Francis Newbolt summed up its advantages in the following passages:

> "By a simple scheme one of the main difficulties of the costly traditional fight between partisan experts can often be got rid of. In the commonest type of case a lawyer had to decide between conflicting specialists, equally competent and confident, and the expense was of course enormous. In rare cases the [official] referees may still have to do this, but it nearly always happens that in a discussion in chambers on date and mode of trial both parties agree that one expert engaged and paid by both sides is preferable."[11]

> "An independent witness surveys the subject matter unbiased and estimates the amount due before any of the great expense of the trial is incurred, with any necessary reservations where questions of law may arise, and he gives a proof to both sides and receives half his fee from each, both halves being made costs in the cause. He may be cross-examined by both parties if either calls him at the trial, which he attends only if required; and both parties retain the right to call any amount of evidence to contradict him, a right which in practice however is not often exercised."[12]

### The court expert

9–09    The informal procedure described by Sir Francis Newbolt in the above passages was in 1934 formally brought within the powers of the High Court by the introduction of what is now Order 40. No doubt the example of the practice of the official referees' courts led to this innovation. By Order 40, rule 1(1) in any cause or matter which is to be tried without a jury and in which any question for an expert witness arises the court may at any time, on the application of any party, appoint an independent expert or, if more than one such question arises, two or more such experts, to inquire and report upon any question of fact or opinion not involving questions of law or of construction. The court expert is if possible to be a person nominated by the parties, and failing agreement to be nominated by the court: rule 1(2). The question to be submitted to the court expert and the instructions (if any) to be given to him must, failing agreement between the parties, be settled by the court: rule 1(3). The court expert's report is sent to the court (together

[11] (1923) 39 L.Q.R. 436.
[12] (1923) 39 L.Q.R. 437.

with such number of copies thereof as the court may direct) and the official referee's clerk sends copies to the parties or their solicitors: rule 2(1). By rule 2(2) the court may direct the expert to make a further or supplementary report, and by the rule 2(3): "any part of a court expert's report which is not accepted by all the parties to the cause or matter in which it is made shall be treated as information furnished to the court and be given such weight as the court thinks fit." Rule 3 deals with experiments and tests and by rule 4 any party may apply for leave to cross-examine and such leave may be given for cross-examination either at the trial or before an examiner. In the official referee's court an examiner would not be used; any pre-trial cross-examination would be conducted before the official referee himself. Rule 5 provides for the fixing of the court expert's fees and for the joint and several liability of the parties to pay them.

### The court expert's evidence

The court expert's report is evidence in the case. It may be accepted **9–10** by the parties, in which event no further question arises. If it is challenged, the above-mentioned procedure for cross-examination will be followed. A party is also at liberty, upon giving notice, to call one expert of his own; he may not call more than one save by leave of the court which will not be granted save in exceptional circumstances: rule 6. The party calling his own expert will also need to obtain the ordinary leave as mentioned in paragraph 9–02, above. If controversy arises and the parties call their own experts it seems desirable that the court expert should be present during the trial and available to give evidence, but *quaere* whether he can be called by the court or otherwise than in compliance with rule 4. His report is, of course, before the court: rule 2(3) as mentioned in paragraph 9–09, above.

The editors of *The Supreme Court Practice* state that applications under Order 40 have been very few in numbers "excepting orders by official referees."[13] These too in recent years have been very few in numbers. More widespread use of this machinery might well reduce the costs of litigation in the official referees' courts. And the Official Referees Users Committee is currently studying whether greater use should be made of court experts.[14]

### Expert assessors

Another way of obtaining the opinion of an expert is for the official **9–11** referee to sit with an expert as assessor. Very little use is however made of this procedure. See paragraph 13–06 below.

---

[13] *The Supreme Court Practice 1988*, para. 40/1–6/2 (which also gives an account of the procedure for fixing and paying the experts' fees).
[14] First Report of O.R. Users Committee, para. 7.

# Chapter 10
# The Scott Schedule

### Origin

**10–01**     George Alexander Scott, barrister-at-law, was an official referee from 1920 to 1933. Confronted, as all official referees have been, with the necessity of rendering manageable disputes involving a long series of complex and controversial facts, he devised the method of arrangement and pleading to which his name has since become attached. The device is sometimes termed an "official referees' schedule" but the more common usage "Scott Schedule" has the merit of deservedly commemorating its inventor.[1]

### Principle of the Schedule

**10–02**     Where the parties are contesting a long catalogue of separate facts the ascertainment of their respective cases by the conventional method of particulars and further and better particulars attached to their respective pleadings becomes irksome to a degree proportional to their length. It was to obviate the searching to and fro through voluminous bundles of pleadings, and to have the issues clearly set out in one document, that G. A. Scott invented his schedule. Basically the scheme is to set out each item seriatim and to append in columns across the sheet the comments of each party. It involves the initial preparation of the schedule by one of the parties and its transmission to the other party or parties for them to make the necessary entries setting out their case or cases. The nature of the schedule will vary according to the nature of the contest. Crucial to the proper construction of the document is the settling of the column headings.

---

[1] Note the spelling: it is not, as is sometimes written, a Scotch Schedule or a Scott's Schedule.

## An illustration

Precedents of Scott Schedules are set out in Appendix D, below. The **10–03** process of constructing such a schedule can be illustrated by taking as an example a contested claim by a landlord against his former tenant for damages for breach of covenant to repair. Such dilapidations cases frequently figure in the official referees' lists and give rise to the simplest as well as one of the commonest forms of Scott Schedule. The document in a case of this kind will consist of six columns and as many lines as there are items of alleged disrepair. In the first column is given the item number, in numerical sequence. This is essential for quick reference during the hearing. Sometimes draftsmen split up their schedule into sections, designated by letters or Roman numerals; in a dilapidations case there might be a separate section for each room in the relevant building. This further facilitates reference, but if it is followed it will be found more satisfactory to keep to the same numerical order from beginning to end rather than to start again at number 1 at each new section. The second column will have some such heading as "Plaintiff's Description of Dilapidations" and in it the plaintiff will succinctly describe each item. Cases of this nature are usually preceded by the service of a schedule pursuant to section 146 of the Law of Property Act 1925, and the descriptions are often taken from that schedule as prepared by the plaintiff's surveyor. The third column will give the amount which the plaintiff claims the repair of the item will cost. This concludes the plaintiff's part of the schedule, and his solicitors will next despatch it to the defendant's solicitors. The next two columns will respectively give the defendant's answer or comment on each item, and the defendant's estimate of the cost of repair. The defendant's comments should be particular; *i.e.* the defendant's case as to the item in question only, and not general. Any general defence, *e.g.* that the defendant is not liable on the covenants, or that the claim is statute barred, will appear in the pleaded defence and need not be repeated. One sometimes sees Scott Schedules to which a cautious pleader has added a note referring to such general defences, but this is unnecessary: it is understood that giving particulars in the Scott Schedule of the defendant's case on each item is without prejudice to any such general defence. Likewise it is understood that specifying a price in column 5 is without prejudice to any assertion in column 4 that the item of repair is denied. If however the disrepair is admitted in column 5 to exist but to be of less extent than alleged by the plaintiff in column 2, it should be made clear whether the price in column 5 is the price for the repair as alleged by the plaintiff or as admitted by the defendant. The sixth and last column in this schedule is left blank, and headed "For official referee's use."

71

## Utility of the Scott Schedule

**10–04**     Apart from its mechanical advantages at the hearing, the Scott Schedule serves a useful purpose in concentrating both parties' attention on the points of agreement and of difference. This facilitates discussion with a view to settlement, or partial settlement. It allows the plaintiff to apprehend what the defendant's case is in detail; and when the differences between the prices respectively advanced by the parties are examined it enables them in many cases to reach a sensible agreement on amounts where the divergence is not great and to concentrate the contest on the instances of larger divergence. At the trial the document will be before the judge and both parties, and the surveyors' evidence on each item is thereby shortened and note-taking facilitated. Anyone who has endeavoured to link evidence with pleadings in the conventional bundle of further and better particulars will have occasion to bless the name of G. A. Scott. Indeed judges find that if for some reason a case of this kind comes to trial without a Scott Schedule they often have to construct one for themselves in order to marshal the evidence and apprehend its effect.

## Cases requiring two Scott Schedules

**10–05**     In some official referee cases it may be desirable to employ two Scott schedules. This state of affairs arises for example in the class of building case, common in the official referees' lists, where a builder is claiming against his customer for his charges and the customer is counterclaiming in respect of allegedly defective work. If the building work was contracted to be charged on a daywork basis or otherwise at reasonable rates, a Scott Schedule will be called for setting out the items of work done and the charges claimed.[2] This Scott Schedule will be prepared by the builder and answered by the customer. The second Scott Schedule will be devised by the customer and answered by the builder and will set out the items of work said to be defective together with the costs of remedying the same.[3]

## Multiple litigants

**10–06**     In the not infrequent cases where a plaintiff sues a number of defendants in respect of the same transaction, a Scott Schedule may be called for with extra columns devoted to the cases of the different defendants. Thus a building owner may be suing three defendants—his architect, his builder, and his builder's sub-contractor. The Scott Schedule will in such a case have a column or pair of columns for each of the defendants,

---

[2] The same considerations will apply where there is a lump sum building contract but the builder claims for a number of extras.
[3] See Form 2, Appendix D below.

and the plaintiff will be required to state against which defendant each item of claim is directed; it is a convenient device to have this indicated in a separate column specifying first and/or second and/or third defendant as the case may be.[4] Similarly if in a Scott Schedule case a defendant brings in one or more third parties he may be ordered by the third party Order for Directions to serve on the third party a copy of the schedule with added columns indicating which of the items are being passed on to the third party and for that third party's answer to the relevant allegations.

## Rejoinder

A case may arise in which the defendant's answers to the plaintiff's entries are such that it becomes desirable to record the plaintiff's comments on these answers. Such cases are not common, but they do occur, and the official referee may then be asked, by ad hoc summons or on an adjourned summons for directions or by agreement to order that a further column be added to the schedule and that the plaintiff append his comments upon the defendant's case within a specified time.

**10–07**

## Other cases

The Scott Schedule is adaptable to a great diversity of situations. Examples occurring regularly are: (i) sale of goods by instalments, where deliveries or payments are disputed[5]; (ii) claims for professional fees, where time spent or work done needs to be specified; (iii) claims for agents' commission; (iv) claims for work done in batches, as in the garment trade; (v) ship repairing cases.

**10–08**

## Column headings

In straightforward cases the drafting of the column headings need present no difficulty. In complicated cases however they may need careful consideration in order that they may require the setting out of the litigant's real case. Where it is anticipated that the items will figure in other documents to be introduced in evidence at the trial it is desirable to add a column giving the appropriate cross references. Thus in sale of goods cases a column should in appropriate cases give the date and serial number of any relevant invoice, and in building cases where an architect's specification or bills of quantities are to be introduced in evidence a column giving the reference to the appropriate sub-paragraph or item number in the other document is desirable. If this is not done, counsel and the judge will probably have to add the references by hand

**10–09**

[4] See Form 2, Appendix D below.
[5] See Form 3, Appendix D below.

73

during the trial, and time and money is saved by having the task performed beforehand.

### Procedure

**10–10** The question whether or not to order a Scott Schedule is one which will be in the official referee's mind at the hearing of the first summons for directions. In an appropriate case the parties or one of them should suggest it; failing this it may be anticipated that the official referee will himself raise the question. It is partly so that this matter may be examined that the Practice Direction[6] requires the nature of the claim and of the defence to be stated at the hearing of the first summons for directions. One matter to be considered in reaching the decision whether or not to make the order is the number of items to be listed. If there are less than, say, six of these it will be as convenient to deal with them by the conventional particulars, but where the number exceeds ten a Scott Schedule is certainly called for. In practice some Scott Schedules run to many hundreds of items. The order made will specify who is first to settle the Scott Schedule and by what date it should be delivered to the other party or parties. It will then require the other parties to complete their portions and re-deliver to the originator within a further secified time. Ordinarily the judge will order a Scott Schedule in general terms, such as "Scott Schedule of items of claim, priced, 28 days; defendant's comments 28 days" thus leaving it to the parties to devise the column headings. If however the parties cannot agree upon the headings, the court will in an appropriate case settle them itself, and in an unusual case may do so in any event. The official referees' court regards the Scott Schedule entries as particulars within the meaning of Order 18, rule 12 and will accordingly in suitable cases order further particulars of the entries if they appear to be insufficient: Order 18, rule 12(3) As to the enforcement of orders see Chapter 12 below.

### The mechanics

**10–11** It is the duty of the party who is directed to initiate the Scott Schedule to see that its various stages are completed and to prepare the final copies for the use of the court and the parties. Unless very short the Schedule should be prepared on brief-sized paper; each sheet should be numbered. The number of copies should be sufficient for each party to have at least three—one each for counsel, solicitor and expert witness, and more may be needed if leading counsel and/or more than one expert are involved. As to the court copy, it is usual and desirable that this be delivered to the judge's clerk before the trial starts, and preferably as soon as may be after completion; it is one of the documents the

---

[6] See para. 8–04 above and Appendix C below.

judges like to look at before embarking on the case, and if a view is to be held it is important that the judge be in possession of his copy before the view takes place. As to the use of the Scott Schedule during the trial, see Chapter 13 below.

# Chapter 11
# Other Interlocutory Orders

### Interlocutory orders

**11–01**    This Chapter deals with some of the miscellaneous interlocutory orders commonly met with in the official referees' chambers and mentions procedures special to the court. It does not pretend to be comprehensive. The official referees possess all the powers and duties of a High Court judge for the purpose of disposing of *inter alia* any interlocutory application[1] and they deal with such everyday matters as further and better particulars of pleadings in the same way as the Masters of the Queen's Bench Division. The official referees' special practices as to Scott Schedules and experts' reports have been dealt with in the last two preceding chapters.

### Discovery

**11–02**    Under Order 24 of the Rules of the Supreme Court discovery may take place automatically pursuant to rule 2, which requires parties to exchange lists of documents within 14 days after close of pleadings, or it may be ordered by the court pursuant to rule 3. The official referees like to order discovery and inspection of documents by dates which fit into their timetable for the progression of the case towards trial. In direct procedure cases, or if a case is remitted in good time, the first summons for directions may well be heard before close of pleadings, indeed it is often heard before defence is delivered. But if there is delay in applying for remission the parties may be in default under rule 2 if they wait for the official referee's Order for Directions. The only immediate sanction for such a default would be an application to strike out under rule 16 and this would be unlikely to produce more than an order to deliver lists. However such a default is taken into account if the court has to

---

[1] Ord. 36, r.4(1)(*a*): see Appendix B below.

consider at a later stage whether to strike out for want of prosecution. In *McVeigh* v. *Tarmac Roadstone Holdings Ltd.* Brandon L.J. said[2]:

> "We were told by counsel that it is common practice as I understand it, in actions of this kind which are likely to be tried by one of the judges taking official referees' business to leave over the question of discovery until the judge concerned is asked to give directions. I do not know whether that is the practice or not. If it is the practice it is inconsistent with the Rules of Court which are applicable and it ought to cease, because the duty of the plaintiff and the defendant is to comply with Order 24, rule 2 unless absolved from doing so by some order of the court."

The delay in that case in giving discovery was given effect to by the Court of Appeal in deciding whether to strike out for want of prosecution, and the dictum of Brandon L.J. may serve to emphasise the importance of quickly taking out the first summons for directions.

### Futher discovery

Complex construction disputes generate a daunting mass of documentation and the official referees are not infrequently asked to order discovery of lines of documentation not hitherto disclosed. They have no hesitation in appropriate cases in ordering discovery supported by affidavit. They may also sometimes be induced to listen sympathetically to applications that documents be listed by files instead of by individual specification where there are many hundreds or even thousands of such papers.

**11–03**

### Views

The viewing of the subject-matter of the dispute is a practice frequently employed by the official referees. It has been found by experience that the viewing by the judge of premises which are alleged to be dilapidated or to have been defectively constructed saves the parties costs and facilitates and shortens proceedings. Views of plant or machinery are also had where desirable. The parties should carefully consider when is the most appropriate time for such a view. If the condition of the premises or plant is to be altered, as by repair, it is desirable if not essential to have a view before the alteration or repair takes place, and an application for a view should be made on the first hearing of the summons for directions or by ad hoc summons when the question of repair emerges. Ordinarily the judges like to hold a view within a few weeks before the hearing date. From the judge's viewpoint this ensures that the impressions derived from the view are fresh in the

**11–04**

---

[2] February 6, 1981, C.A. (unrep.).

mind when the case is opened, and from the parties' standpoint the attendance of clients, legal advisers, and expert witnesses at the *locus in quo* may form a valuable part of preparing for trial. Sometimes views are had during the course of the trial; this is less valuable and usually arises either because the court is sitting away from London and in the vicinity of the *locus*, or because it has become apparent during the hearing that a view is desirable and ought to have been ordered previously. No charge is made by the court for a view, and the judges are willing to attend such in any part of the country. A view may be ordered on the original or adjourned summons for directions or on an ad hoc summons; the convenience of the parties will be consulted as to date and time. The judge will not ordinarily require the attendance of any particular persons, save to ensure that all parties concerned are, or have the opportunity to be, represented, but it has been found in practice that if it is building work that is to be inspected the attendance of the various parties' surveyors is desirable. At the view the judge will wish to have pointed out to him any features to which any party attaches importance, but he will strictly discourage any attempts to argue differing viewpoints. The utility of views lies not only in informing the mind of the court but also in bringing together the persons concerned in the presence of the features complained of: in building cases it not infrequently happens that a settlement of the action follows upon the holding of a view.

### Evidence

**11–05**    Expert evidence is dealt with in Chapter 9, above. In addition to the ordinary orders as to affidavit evidence and the like, the official referees have pioneered the practice of requiring the exchange of proofs before trial. Originally this could only be ordered by consent, but by a 1986 amendment to the Rules of the Supreme Court the official referees, together with the Admiralty Court, the Commercial Court and the Chancery Division, are empowered to enforce such disclosure. By Order 38, rule 2A, an official referee may, if he thinks fit for the purpose of disposing fairly and expeditiously of the cause or matter and saving costs, direct any party to serve on the other parties written statements of the oral evidence which the party intends to lead on any issue of fact to be decided at the trial. The order may be conditional; it usually provides for exchange of statements about six weeks before trial and that the party should serve a copy of his statements on the court. If the party serving the statement does not call the witness the other party may put the statement in evidence. If the witness is called he may not give evidence beyond his statement unless the court gives leave or it relates to new matters which have arisen in the course of the trial. The court may, and usually does, order that the statement shall stand as the witness's evidence in chief.[2a]

The official referees will not ordinarily make an order for the examination by an examiner or commissioner of a witness who is unable to attend court by reason of infirmity or intention to go abroad: they prefer to hear the evidence themselves and will appoint a time and place for this to take place.

## Other interlocutory orders

Frequent among the summonses in the official referees' lists are the following. **11–06**

### 1. *Applications to amend pleadings*

The complexity of building disputes is such that few actions reach trial without amendments to the pleadings. The court may be expected to accede to such applications upon the usual terms, *i.e.* leave to other parties to make consequential amendments and costs of and occasioned by the amendments to be the other party's in any event.

### 2. *Applications for security for costs*

Where the plaintiff is ordinarily resident out of the jurisdiction[3] or where a plaintiff company is thought to be unable to pay the costs of the defendant if the claim fails[4] application may be made for security for costs. In the Companies Act cases the official referees like to have the evidence of lack of means given by affidavit, and in both cases it is advantageous to the applicant to put in a draft bill of costs. One feature recurring in the official referees' court is that of the plaintiff builder or sub-contractor whose main or only asset is the prospect of success in the action; the judge then is faced with the alternative of ordering security, which may unjustly stop the action because the plaintiff cannot provide it, or of refusing security, which may unjustly penalise a successful defendant. Such cases turn upon the judge's view of the prospects of success or failure and raise problems similar to those arising on Order 14 applications. The parties in these cases can help the court by providing any evidence tending to show that the claim is either specious or well-founded.[5]

### 3. *Applications by solicitors to be taken off the record*

By Order 67, rule 6 where a party has not given notice of change of solicitor, a solicitor who has ceased to act may apply to the court for an

---

[2a] See para. 9–12 n. 3a above.
[3] Ord. 23, r.1.
[4] Companies Act 1985, s.726(1).
[5] See *Sir Lindsay Parkinson & Co. Ltd.* v. *Triplan Ltd.* [1973] Q.B. 609.

order declaring that fact. The application is to "the court" and in official referees business this means to the assigned official referee. This is mentioned here because solicitors sometimes in official referee cases make such applications to a Master, who may be led into making an order without having jurisdiction to do so.[6] It may be that the profession is misled in this regard because notice of change of solicitor has to be filed not in the official referee's office but in the Central Office.[7] Although there is no requirement so to do, it is highly desirable that a copy of the notice of change should be handed to the clerk to the assigned official referee.

### 4. *Applications to dismiss for want of prosecution*

Owing to their complexity the bigger construction cases take a considerable time to come to trial and the official referees are from time to time faced with applications to strike out because of inordinate delay. Such applications have markedly diminished in number since the decision of the House of Lords in *Birkett* v. *James*.[8] When they do occur the official referees may be expected to appreciate that the time scale in such cases is inevitably longer than in simpler litigation.

### 5. *Applications for interim payments*

These must be made to a judge other than the one assigned: see paragraph 8–09, above.

### Third party proceedings

11–07    Where the whole case, as distinct from an issue or issues, is referred to the official referees, they have control of all ancillary matters[9] and any application such as for leave to issue third party proceedings must be made to them and not to the Master. Third party proceedings are common in the construction cases which form the staple of official referees' business. If a defendant's third party notice is issued before serving his defence he needs no leave[10] but otherwise he must obtain the leave of the official referee to whom his case has been assigned. Application for this leave is made *ex parte* and must be supported by an affidavit stating (a) the nature of the claim made by the plaintiff in the action, (b) the stage which the proceedings in the action have reached, (c) the nature of the claim made by the applicant or particulars of the question or issue required to be determined, as the case may be, and the facts on which

---

[6] See *Durston* v. *O'Keefe* [1974] 1 W.L.R. 775, and para. 7–05 above.
[7] Ord. 67, r.1(2).
[8] [1978] A.C. 297.
[9] See para. 7–06 above.
[10] Ord. 16, r.1(2).

the proposed third party notice is based, and (d) the name and address of the person against whom the third party notice is too be issued.[11] The practice is to leave this affidavit with the official referee's clerk; the judge will then consider it and in the ordinary case will indorse his leave upon the affidavit. In unusual circumstances however he may require a summons to be issued[12] and will hear the parties before deciding whether or not to give leave. A summons might be required for instance if the third party proceedings are proposed at a late stage in the action, when the date of trial has already been fixed, and a question would arise whether the existing parties would be prejudiced by delay or otherwise if leave were given.

### Third party summons for directions

Once third party proceedings are commenced the third party sum- **11–08** mons for directions must be taken out before the official referee con- cerned. If a summons in the main action is pending it will be wise to ask for the third party summons to be heard at the same time. The judges like to have all the parties before them on such occasions because those who are not parties to the third party proceedings are nevertheless jointly concerned in such matters as experts' reports, the Scott Schedule, and the trial date. The judge may require the Scott Schedule to be extended and completed by a third party; he may require service of experts' reports upon all parties; and he will fix the trial date with the representations of all parties in mind. The third party in an ordinary case will be given leave to appear and take part in the trial of the action, and to have the third party proceedings tried together with the main action—or as a separate issue, as convenience dictates.

### Long summonses

A feature of the practice in recent years has been the growth in long **11–09** summonses. These are defined as being expected to last for 15 minutes or over and are heard on Fridays. They are often of considerable com- plexity, as may be illustrated by the recent case of *Imodco Ltd.* v. *Wimpey Major Products Ltd.*[13] There the plaintiffs applied for an Order 14 judg- ment alternatively for an order for an interim payment under Order 29, while the defendants applied for a stay under an arbitration clause. The senior official referee's decision to order both an interim payment and a stay led to a difference of opinion in the Court of Appeal.

---

[11] Ord. 16, r.2(2).
[12] Ord. 16, r.2(1).
[13] December 18, 1987, C.A. (unrep.).

# Chapter 12
# Preparing for Trial

### The time table

**12–01**    As has been indicated[1] the official referees attach importance to the proper spacing out of the interlocutory stages of preparation for trial with a view to a smooth progression to a fixed date assigned to the commencement of the hearing. The most important points along this road are the discovery and inspection of documents, the preparation of the Scott Schedule where one is employed, and the mutual disclosure of experts' reports. Often, too, the furnishing of further and better particulars of pleadings assumes an importance in the progression. All these and any other interlocutory steps will have been assigned a date within which they should be accomplished, and the official referees regard it as important that this time table of dates be adhered to. There may be some elasticity in the timetable but if it is not broadly followed, then either the case will commence with one or other or both parties ill-prepared, or one or other or both will be applying to adjourn the hearing. Any such adjournment is to be avoided not only in the interest of whichever party wants his case to be heard but also because it dislocates the official referees' carefully spaced out list.[2]

### The enforcement of orders

**12–02**    Because of the foregoing considerations the official referees are willing to consider the use of their coercive powers in cases where an order is not obeyed in time. There are two weapons in their coercive armoury, the final order and the "unless" order.

---

[1] Paras. 8–06 and 8–07 above.
[2] See para. 13–03 below "Adjournment of trial."

## Final orders and unless orders

A final order may be made upon an application by a party for an **12–03** extension of the time within which he is required to take some step, or upon the application of his opponent. Its effect is as its name implies: the extension given is final and no further time will be given, save in quite exceptional circumstances. If it is not complied with the defaulter is in technical contempt, and his opponent has grounds for applying to strike out his statement of claim or defence as the case may be, and then to obtain judgment. See *per* Diplock L.J. in *Allen* v. *Sir Alfred McAlpine & Sons*[3]:

> "The power to strike out . . . should not be exercised without giving the plaintiff an opportunity of remedying his default unless the court is satisfied either that the default has been intentional and contumelious or [there has been inexcusable delay] . . . Disobedience to a peremptory order of the court would be sufficient to satisfy the first condition."

The unless order is a stricter version of this process and it embodies in one direction both the element of finality and the consequent order for striking out and awarding judgment. A typical unless order reads as follows:

> "Unless the further and better particulars of the defence and counterclaim ordered on the 4th day of October 1978 be served by the 2nd day of January 1979 the defence and counter-claim be struck out and that the plaintiff be at liberty to sign judgment for damages to be assessed."[4]

Although draconian in its effect the object of an unless order is to secure compliance with the court's orders and not to punish: see *Husbands of Marchwood* v. *Drummond Ltd.*[5] In that case the defendants had failed to comply with an order for discovery (not an unless order). The plaintiff took out a summons to debar the defendants from defending. Two days before the hearing of the summons the defendants gave the required discovery. Nevertheless the official referee ordered the defendants to be debarred unless they paid the balance of the claim into court. Upon appeal Russell L.J. said[6]:

> "The condition requiring the payment of the balance into court is something which is quite inappropriate in the sense that it is a punishment which does not fit the crime . . . What should have

---

[3] [1968] 2 Q.B. 229 at 259.
[4] Cited from the judgment of Lawton L.J. in *Samuels* v. *Linzi Dresses Ltd.* [1981] Q.B. 115 at 118.
[5] [1975] 1 W.L.R. 603.
[6] *Ibid.* at 605.

been done . . . was for the plaintiff to ask for an order striking out the defence unless within a certain time the defendants had produced their discovery."

### Relief against unless orders

12–04.    Until recently there has been doubt whether, once a judgment had been signed pursuant to an unless order, it could be set aside for some good reason. The doubt stemmed from the Divisonal Court decision of *Whistler* v. *Hancock*[7] which appeared to decide that once a judgment was signed an action was dead and no court had power to revive it. This question was of particular interest to the official referees' courts because the judges wished in suitable cases to make use of the very effective sanction of the unless order by way of enforcing their timetable, but at the same time were hesitant to do so if there was thereafter no *locus poenitentiae* because grave injustice might result where the order had been transgressed inadvertently or without real fault. In *R.* v. *Bloomsbury and Marylebone County Court, ex p. Villerwest Ltd.*[8] Lord Denning M.R. had indicated that *Whistler* v. *Hancock* had outlived its usefulness,[9] and following this dictum two official referee cases allowed relief against judgments upon unless orders in appropriate circumstances. The first of these was *R. Laws Plan Build Ltd.* v. *Globe Picture Theatres (Bristol) Ltd.*[10] There a solicitor had endeavoured to comply with an unless order to deliver further and better particulars but owing to a mistake in his office the particulars although prepared were not enclosed with the covering letter and by the time the mistake had been discovered the other party had signed judgment. Upon application speedily made the official referee set aside the judgment, holding that the object of the unless order was discipline and not punishment[11] and that justice required no greater penalty than that the defaulter should pay the costs thrown away. The other case was *Samuels* v. *Linzi Dresses Ltd.*[12] There a defendant had failed to comply with an order requiring him to furnish further and better particulars and on December 15, 1978 the official referee made the order cited at paragraph 12–03, above requiring compliance by January 2, 1979. However despite work by both solicitor and counsel over the Christmas holiday the pleading was not finalised in time because certain factual gaps in counsel's draft called for further

[7] (1878) 3 Q.B.D. 83.
[8] [1976] 1 W.L.R. 362.
[9] *Ibid.* at 366.
[10] (1978) 8 Build. L.R. 29.
[11] *Cf. per* Stamp L.J. in *Husbands of Marchwood Ltd.* v. *Drummond Ltd.* [1975] 1 W.L.R. 603 at 606: "I think Order 24, rule 16(1) is designed to secure compliance with the rules and orders of the court relating to discovery and not to punish a party for not having complied with them within the time limited for the purpose."
[12] [1981] Q.B. 115.

instructions from the clients, whose office was shut down during the week following Christmas. The defendants applied to extend the time; the plaintiff pleaded *Whistler* v. *Hancock*; the official referee held that he had jurisdiction to extend time and in the exercise of his discretion he did so. The plaintiff appealed, and the Court of Appeal at last delivered the quietus to *Whistler* v. *Hancock*: it was held to be inconsistent with the Rules of the Supreme Court and to have been wrong in the first place.[13] The law is now clear and is set forth in this passage from the judgment of Roskill L.J.[14]:

> "In my judgment therefore the law today is that a court has power to extend the time where an unless order has been made but not been complied with; but that it is a power which should be exercised cautiously and with due regard to the necessity for maintaining the principle that orders are made to be complied with and not to be ignored. Primarily it is a question for the discretion of the master or the judge in chambers whether the necessary relief should be granted or not."

**Peremptory orders: practice**

The power to make final and unless orders is derived from the inher- **12–05** ent power of the court to control its proceedings, and also in a number of instances from the express provisions of the Rules of the Supreme Court. Thus in the case of discovery of documents it is provided by Order 24, rule 16(1) that in the case of default "the court may make such order as it thinks just including, in particular, an order that the action be dismissed or, as the case may be, an order that the defence be struck out and judgment be entered accordingly." Other relevant provisions are Order 19, rule 1 (default of pleadings) and Order 26, rule 6 (default as to interrogatories). There is no express provision as regards the common case of default in giving further and better particulars but in this instance and in the case of entries in the Scott Schedule the official referees rely on Order 18, rule 12(3) empowering them to order particulars "on such terms as the court thinks just."[15] The peremptory orders may be made upon an ad hoc summons taken out under the appropriate rule, or may be made upon any relevant summons, such as an adjourned summons for directions or a time summons. Where an unless order is made it will ordinarily provide not only for the striking out of the offender's pleading but also provide for judgment. Where made in favour of a plaintiff this will be judgment for the amount claimed, if liquidated, or for damages to be assessed if the claim is unliquidated,

---

[13] *Ibid.* at 127.
[14] *Ibid.* at 126–127.
[15] See *Davey* v. *Bentinck* [1893] 1 Q.B. 185.

and also for costs to be taxed if not agreed and, where asked for, for interest on the judgment, to be assessed.

### Setting aside judgment: practice

**12–06**    Where the time limited in an unless order has been overrun and the other party has signed judgment the defaulting party may apply to set aside the judgment. But (*a*) he must have some good explanation of the failure to comply, and (b) he must apply promptly. No better instances can be given of the kinds of grounds which would found a successful application than those existing in the two cases mentioned in paragraph 12–04, above of *R. Laws Plan Build Ltd.* v. *Globe Picture Theatres (Bristol) Ltd.* and *Samuels* v. *Linzi Dresses Ltd.* The mitigating facts must be put on affidavit and the disobeyed order must now be able to be complied with forthwith. Speed is essential: a summons taken out, say, a month after the due date is unlikely to be met with a favourable reception. Either delay or lack of convincing merit will defeat the application, bearing in mind the above-mentioned words of Roskill L.J. that the power to set aside should be exercised cautiously.[16] Nor can an unsuccessful applicant get round his difficulty by issuing a fresh writ; it will be dismissed as an abuse of the process of the court unless there are grounds similar to those exemplified in *Samuel* v. *Linzi Dresses* for exercising a discretion in his favour: *Janov* v. *Morris.*[17] If the application to set aside judgment is granted the other party will be awarded costs in any event. Express power to set aside is conferred by Order 19, rule 9 (pleadings), Order 24, r. 17 (discovery) and Order 26, rule 8 (interrogatories).

### Preparing papers

**12–07**    Once the tackle is in order the parties' solicitors will need to consider the arrangement of the papers for the hearing. Papers readily retrievable and handily arranged ensure a saving of time and consequently of costs at the hearing. In a small case all that is needed is a bundle of pleadings, a bundle of relevant correspondence and loose copies of the two experts' reports. But in the larger building and engineering cases greater elaboration is called for. There is no class of litigation today which produces more paper than a building dispute, and when such a case is being tried an official referee's court will seem to be submerged in a sea of folders, binders, drawings and papers of all kinds. Here it is necessary for the parties' solicitors, in collaboration if possible, to devote considerable thought to the problem of arrangement. The object of this exercise is to have any document readily to hand, whether it be

[16] See para. 12–04 above.
[17] [1981] 1 W.L.R. 1389.

the hand of the judge, of counsel, or of expert witness. To this end documents of ordinary size should be filed in ring binders; this is desirable because no such case is ever tried without fresh documents, hitherto thought irrelevant, being needed; these can then be copied (there are speedy facilities for document copying available to the official referees' courts in London; application should be made to the court usher) and inserted in the ring binder in proper chronological order and given an "a" number. A problem is whether to put all documents in one series of binders in chronological order or whether to attempt to classify. This must depend on the subject-matter: thus sometimes it is useful to separate contemporary reports, site minutes and site diaries and the like from the correspondence. But whether separate or not the golden rule is that all documents must be arranged in chronological order and must be consecutively numbered. In one of the large construction industry cases there will then be separate bundles containing (i) pleadings, (ii) contemporary documents, (iii) experts reports. Class (ii) may well run into many binders and may as indicated above be sub-divided into correspondence and other documents. Outsize documents present their own problems. Firstly, drawings: many official referee's cases involve the perusal of a quantity of plans, sections, elevations and other drawings which are of necessity large in size and cumbersome to handle. They should never be rolled: however handy this is elsewhere it leads only to confusion in court. They should be folded to approximately foolscap size and so folded that the drawing number, which is usually in the bottom right-hand corner, is on top. They should then be arranged in numerical order and kept together as may be convenient in a box or large folder or simply with rubber bands. Finally, the Scott Schedule: this is often as large in area as the architects' drawings, but it must not be dissected, nor folded more than once, otherwise there is lost the central object of the schedule which is to present the parties' views at a glance in one spread. It may run to very many sheets; these should be clipped together and left at that.

## Papers for the court

In short cases the official referees like to have the papers a day or two **12–08** before the trial is due to commence so that they may shorten proceedings by reading the pleadings and correspondence beforehand. These papers should be delivered to the judge's clerk as soon as is convenient. But in the long and complicated cases this process is out of the question and the judge will wait to be guided by counsel in finding his way about the multifarious papers. Solicitors in such cases should keep in touch with the judge's clerk with a view to delivering the documentation to court in good time so that the commencement of the hearing may not be delayed. Often it will be possible to place the material in the court room on the evening before the case starts.

### Pre-trial conference

**12–09**     In complex cases it is desirable to hold a pre-trial conference several weeks before the trial date. Technically this meeting is a hearing for further directions. It is sometimes suggested by the court and sometimes procured by the parties. Ordinarily it becomes manifest upon the hearing of the summons for directions whether the case is one of those which will benefit from such a meeting, and the summons for directions is adjourned to a suitable date for this purpose. Alternatively a party may procure such a meeting by taking out a summons for further directions: in this case he must be careful to see that any third party proceedings are also activated since all interested parties ought to be present. The main object of this meeting is to discuss and if possible lay down a programme so that parties and their experts need not be present when parts of the case which do not concern them are being tried. The class of case in which this procedure is of particular utility is that in which there are many separate and often unconnected issues—the counterclaim may raise questions differing from those raised by the claim, and third parties may be involved in some but not in other issues, while special defences such as that of limitation may affect some parties and not others. One aim of the official referee at a pre-trial conference will be to disentangle issues which can be tried separately, albeit as part of the continuous hearing of the case. This saves time by making it easier for all concerned to grapple with the matters in hand and saves costs by avoiding unnecessary attendances. The judge will also be willing to assist on other programme matters such as the setting aside of days for expert witnesses on both sides to be heard. One cost-saving device which sometimes emerges from a pre-trial conference is the use of a sampling procedure, whereby a representative selection of items in a lengthy Scott Schedule is singled out for initial trial. The decision upon these may well influence the parties to reach agreement as to the remaining schedule issues.

# Chapter 13
# The Hearing

### The fixed date

Virtually all official referee cases are assigned a fixed date for hearing **13–01** either on the original or on the adjourned summons for directions. The parties are required to specify a realistic estimated length for the trial. Owing to pressure on the official referees' lists, the date may be 9 to 12 months or more ahead. This interval is satisfactory for the longer construction cases where indeed in some instances more than 12 months is needed for the inspecting, sifting and arranging of the great mass of documentation as well as for securing dates convenient to specialist counsel and experts. If a longer interval is needed it is likely to be granted. But it is appreciated by the official referees that their simpler cases ought to be tried more speedily; how far this can be achieved depends on how well the increased number of courts operated can relieve the pressure.

### Transfer to another judge

Formerly the judge to whom the case was assigned was the judge **13–02** who would try it. In those days each official referee had a manageable list. In those days cases were shorter, settlements were fewer and the official referee could space the work out and attend to all his own cases. They were personal to him, as an arbitrator's case is personal today, and the system reflected the origins of the official referees as official arbitrators. This identity of the judge with the case still operates in the majority of instances, but the increase in the inflow of work together with an increase in the settlement rate has made inroads upon this principle. In the 1960s the annual intake of cases increased from 200 to 400 and by 1976 it was 633. Ten years later, in 1986, it was 1,105 but the number of judges had doubled from three to six. However, the number of cases tried out had not doubled, a fact emphasising the longer and more complicated nature of the cases now coming before the court. The excess work has been accommodated by lengthening the time awaiting trial, by employing deputy judges in extra courts, and by deliberately overburdening the lists.[1] In order to dispose of the lists without quite inordinate delays it has become the practice to double or treble book each official referee's time. By the time that the trial date arrives settlements will usually have seen to it that the assigned official referee is free, but if this is not the case one of his colleagues may have found that all his cases have settled, and the case will be transferred to him. If no other official referee is available the circuit administrator will be asked to find a deputy, who will ordinarily be either an active or a retired circuit judge whom the Lord Chancellor then nominates to do official referee's business pursuant to section 68(1) of the Supreme Court Act 1981. Transfer from one judge to another is effected in the office pursuant to Order 36, rule 7(2): "Any official referee may order the transfer of any business from himself to any other official referee who consents to the transfer." Very occasionally no judge can be found available when the fixed date arrives and the case has to be postponed. This is a most unfortunate occurrence and one causing hardship to litigants; but it is rare and it is difficult to see how it can be avoided. Meanwhile the meeting of fixed dates by transfer from one judge to another represents a step away from the original conception of the arbitrator-judge towards the official referees as a body acting as a division rather as the Commercial Court does.

In addition to transfer by consent of the judge there remains in the rules a power to the Lord Chancellor or the Lord Chief Justice to make a transfer order "If it is expedient so to do having regard to the state of the business pending before the official referees."[2] This rule has been used rarely if at all since the simpler consensual transfer procedure was introduced.

### Adjournment of trial

**13–03**   Because the dates are fixed the court does not look with favour upon applications to vacate a trial date, particularly if made not long before the hearing is due to commence. If the parties agree, however, such adjournments are usually granted, but if the application is opposed a strong case will have to be made out. The parties must appreciate that if another date has to be found in the future the effect will be to postpone the hearing for approximately 9 to 12 months. The application to adjourn is made by summons; sometimes unopposed applications can be dealt with in the office and parties' solicitors are advised to consult the judge's clerk as soon as possible.

---

[1] The situation has also been eased by a steady increase in the settlement rate: see the statistics in Appendix F below.
[2] Ord. 36, r. 7(1).

## Venue

The great majority of official referee cases are heard in the official **13–04**
referees' courts in London.[3] Venue may however have been fixed outside London either on the south-eastern circuit (to which the London
official referees are officially attached) at such towns as Brighton or Nor-
wich, or at towns on other circuits if the parties require the services of
the London official referees.[4] Cases where a local venue is indicated are
those with a number of local witnesses where the cost of bringing them
to London becomes a consideration. If local solicitors and experts are
also involved the balance of convenience and economy clearly points to
local trial. The official referees will also in appropriate cases sit locally to
hear evidence or some of the evidence and then adjourn to London. The
official referees' place in the matter of local trial was expressed by Viscount Simon L.C. in *Osenton & Co.* v. *Johnston*[5] in these words:

> "In many cases the need for local trial is appropriately met by fixing
> the place of trial at assizes, but a very long investigation is for prac-
> tical reasons not suited to this treatment whereas an official referee
> can establish himself in the part of the country which is most con-
> venient for the hearing and carry the case to its conclusion, if
> necessary, even though it lasts a long time."

See also *Bannister* v. *McDonald*[6] and the passage in Burrows on "Official
Referees"[7] where he instanced as a typical local venue case a relator
action to establish a right of way over a footpath referred by Clauson J.:
"In pursuance of the judge's order the action was tried in the district
where the path was situated and about 38 witnesses gave evidence. The
parties were thereby saved the expense of bringing the large number of
witnesses to London and the official referee had the advantage of being
able to inspect the path during the hearing."[8]

The parties are not called upon to pay any additional court costs by
reason of the court sitting outside London. All the court's own travell-
ing expenses are defrayed by the Treasury.

## Powers of the court

The official referee's court has the powers of the High Court no less **13–05**
and no more. The belief, formerly held, that an official referee had
wider, arbitral, powers has been overruled by the Court of Appeal in

[3] See para. 5–01 above "Location."
[4] See para. 5–02 above "Sittings outside London," and for sittings of provincial official
referees, see para. 15–08 below.
[5] [1942] A.C. 130 at 135.
[6] [1890] W.N. 50; action for injunction to restrain interference with ancient lights, to be
tried locally.
[7] 56 L.Q.R. 504.
[8] *Ibid.* at 512.

*Crouch's Case.*[9] By Order 36, rule 4(1)(*a*) "the official referee shall for the purpose of disposing of any cause or matter . . . or any other business referred to him have the same jurisdiction powers and duties (including the power of committal and discretion as to costs) as a judge, exercisable or, as the case may be, to be performed as nearly as circumstances admit in the like cases, in the like manner and subject to the like limitations." These powers are expressed to be "subject to any directions contained in the order referring any business to an official referee."[10] However it is not the practice to set any limit to the official referee's powers in the referral order, save in those cases where an issue only is referred, when the jurisdiction is necessarily limited.[11] Consequently the course of ordinary proceedings before an official referee is indistinguishable from the trial of an action in the Queen's Bench or Chancery Divisions. It is possible still however to discern some hint of the informality associated with the arbitral beginnings of the court, although the old practice whereby counsel addressed the court seated has long since been given up.[12] Witnesses however are invited to sit. The above-mentioned rule 4(1)(*a*) expressly confers the power to commit for contempt of court, and the official referee has likewise the power to issue subpoenas.[13]

### Assessors

**13–06**  The modes of trial of High Court matters laid down by Order 33, rule 2 include trial before "an official referee with or without the assistance of assessors." By Order 33, rule 6 a trial with the assistance of assessors "shall take place in such manner and on such terms as the court may direct."[14] Only occasional use is nowadays made of these provisions and the official referees find that in the general run of their cases all the technical assistance they need can be obtained from the parties' experts witnesses.[15] However if some unusual technical matter comes to be litigated the parties might be well advised to bear in mind their right to ask for an assessor. The above-mentioned provisions make it clear that one or more assessors may be appointed. Presumably one would suffice if the parties agreed on his identity or left his selection to the judge but failing agreement two would be appointed, one being nominated or suggested by each of the opposing parties.

---

[9] *Northern Regional Health Authority* v. *Crouch Construction Ltd.* [1984] 1 Q.B. 644, examined at para. 6–08 above.

[10] Ord. 36, r. 4(1).

[11] See para. 7–05 above.

[12] The practice had already been discontinued in 1940 when Sir Roland Burrows wrote on official referees: 56 L.Q.R. 504 at 509.

[13] A subpoena is issued out of the Central Office: Ord. 38, r. 14.

[14] See also s.70 of the Supreme Court Act 1981.

[15] See also para. 9–09 above "The court expert."

## Procedure

By Order 36, rule 4(1)(*b*) "every trial and all other proceedings before **13–07** an official referee shall, as nearly as circumstances admit, be conducted in the like manner as the like proceedings before a judge." Little need be said here about the familiar pattern of opening speech by plaintiff's counsel, the examination, cross-examination and re-examination of the plaintiff's witnesses, and the like for the defendant, followed by closing speeches. The procedure is the same as that followed in the Chancery and Queen's Bench Divisions. The hours however are likely to be more flexible. The normal commencement time is 10.30 a.m. but while the rising time is normally 4.15 p.m. the court will not necessarily adjourn at that time but will consult the parties' wishes, especially if there has been a late start. Nor is it a difficult task to induce an official referee to sit into a vacation to finish a case, and indeed sittings in parts of the Long Vacation are now commonplace.[16] Order 61, rule 6(1) applies the High Court terms to official referees' business, but also provides that "nothing in this rule shall prevent an official referee from sitting in vacation if he thinks it expedient so to do." One unorthodox aspect of procedure, less common now than formerly, is the hearing of two opposing experts alternately on the same day. This is inappropriate in a complex matter but where for example there is a straightforward Scott Schedule of defects or dilapidations setting out opposing experts' views the judge may have both surveyors sworn and then deal with the scheduled items seriatim, taking the evidence of first one and then the other surveyor before passing on to the next item. This is a considerable time-saver. Any other time-saving devices which counsel may propose will be sympathetically considered: as a former official referee said "the true function of the court is . . . not to conciliate or exhort the parties, much less to hurry them . . . but to use the available machinery of litigation to enable them to settle their disputes according to law without grievous waste and unnecessary delay and anxiety."[17]

## Shorthand note

Regarding shorthand notes a remarkable divergence exists between **13–08** the provisions of the Rules of the Supreme Court and the practice in the Royal Courts of Justice. By Order 68, rule 7(1) "if in a reference for trial before an official referee the referee certifies that it is desirable for a shorthand note to be taken, such a note shall be taken of the evidence given orally in court and of any judgment delivered by the referee." But all hearings by official referees in open court in the Royal Courts of

---

[16] See para. 5–04 above "Terms."
[17] Sir Henry Newbolt, "Expedition and Economy in Litigation," (1923) 39 L.Q.R. 427 at 440.

Justice are mechanically recorded[18] and no judge's certificate need be asked for or given. The origin of this practice is not now recalled; it was not in existence at the date of the Evershed Committee's report.[19] However while parties in London need not ask the official referee to exercise his power to order a recording it is otherwise with sittings outside London and parties with venue in the provinces should make application under Order 68, rule 7 for a certificate if they wish to have recorded the judgment or any other part of the hearing. (For the varying practices in different provincial centres, see paragraph 15–10 below). If the official referee so certifies, and in any case in London, the taking of the note is at the public expense, but transcripts have to be paid for unless the matter falls within the provisions of Order 68 as to legal aid cases and impecunious litigants: these provisions are expressly applied to official referees' cases by Order 68, rule 7(2).

### Judgment

**13–09**   Judgments are oral and are frequently reserved. The official referee has the same powers as any other judge in the High Court to make ancillary orders such as to provide for costs, for interest, for stay pending appeal, and the like. As to interest the practice of the Commercial Court to apply realistic rates is generally followed. As to costs, the official referees often endeavour to lighten the burden on the taxing masters by making proportion orders in the frequently occurring class of case where a number of separate issues has been tried and the party who was successful on balance has nevertheless lost on some issues. Such a party will often find the balance of winning and losing reflected in the percentage of his costs which the other party is ordered to pay. The formal order of the court is drawn up by the judge's clerk, sealed by him, and signed by the judge.

### Reports

**13–10**   Dealing as they do with complex contractual situations the official referees frequently find themselves called upon to decide hitherto unexplored points of law. Indeed a surprising number of leading cases will be found to have started in the official referees' courts.[20] But unless appealed the official referees' decisions have until recently only occasionally been reported. The learned editor of *Hudson on Building Contracts* complained of this phenomenon when he spoke of the "universal tendency of the English High Court to refer building and

---

[18] By Ord. 68, r. 8 a mechanical recording is the equivalent of a shorthand note.
[19] Final Report, Cmd. 8878 (1953) para. 527(*d*).
[20] *e.g. Sutcliffe* v. *Thackrah* [1974] A.C. 727; *Gilbert Ash (Northern) Ltd.* v. *Modern Engineering (Bristol) Ltd.* [1974] A.C. 689; *Anns* v. *London Borough of Merton* [1978] A.C. 728.

civil engineering cases to the official referees, whose judgments are unfortunately rarely, if ever, reported, despite their great experience and often excellent judgments."[21] This neglect by the law reporters has led in the past to important decisions being known only to a few specialists who had provided themselves with a copy of the shorthand notes of the judgment. This undesirable state of affairs has however recently been rectified first by the institution in 1976 of the series of *Building Law Reports* (Build.L.R.) whose editors are now publishing those official referee judgments which they deem worthy of recording, including past decisions, and secondly by the commencement in 1985 of the *Construction Law Reports* (Con.L.R.) with the avowed object of reporting official referees' judgments of interest to the construction industry. The editors of this new series state that:

> "We have been concerned that much more attention should be paid to the judgments of the official referees. The official referees' court has now become in effect a specialist construction industry court, one of the few in the world . . . Most of the cases which come before the official referees involve complex and technical issues of fact but may also involve difficult and important questions of law. It is important that the guidance which emerges from the court should be generally available . . . We plan to report all official referees' decisions containing points of construction law."[22]

Decisions are also summarised in the Construction Industry Law Letter and recently the Official Referees' Users Committee has pressed the Law Reports and the All England Law Reports to report more official referees' cases.[23]

---

[21] (10th ed., 1st Supp.) Introduction, p. 2.
[22] Preface to (1985) 1 Con.L.R.
[23] "After meetings with the editors of the Official and All England Reports they each agreed that O.R. judgments should be treated the same as other first instance decisions of the High Court": First Report, Official Referees' Users Committee, para. 8.2.

# Chapter 14
# Appeal

### Appeal to the Court of Appeal

**14–01**     The salient feature of appeals from the judgments and orders of official referees is that, with limited exceptions, there is no appeal on fact. The provisions of Order 58, rule 4 are explicit:

> "(3) Except as provided in paragraph (1)[1] and section 13 of the Administration of Justice Act 1960 (which provides for an appeal in cases of contempt of court), no judgment order or decision of an official referee in relation to any cause matter question or issue ordered to be tried before him shall be called in question by appeal or otherwise."

This strict limitation was introduced by the Administration of Justice Act 1932, presumably because it was thought not to be in the public interest to re-litigate the amount of detail present in a typical official referee case. The innovation was not without its critics. In *Thomas Conway Ltd.* v. *Henwood*[2] Greer L.J. applied the new restriction with reluctance. He said that "a statutory provision which deprived litigating parties of powers of appeal which they had before the statute was passed was a serious alteration of the rights of the parties and he could imagine people thinking that the Administration of Justice Act 1932, unwisely gave to official referees . . . power to decide matters finally." Subsequently an attempt was made to induce the Evershed Committee to recommend the reintroduction of full rights of appeal on fact. That committee devoted three pages of its Final Report to the arguments for and against reintroduction of the right of appeal, and decided that "on balance we do not feel able to support the proposal to restore generally the right of appeal on fact from official referees."[3] They did however recommend that a party should at the time of remission have the right

---

[1] *Sc.* para. (1) of r.4: see Appendix B below.
[2] (1934) 50 T.L.R. 474.
[3] Final Report, 1953, Cmd. 8878, paras. 526–530.

to opt for appeal on fact; this recommendation was not carried into effect. The only way of securing appeal on fact (other than in fraud or professional negligence cases) is to apply to transfer the case to the appropriate Division. Sometimes it has been possible to have the assigned official referee try such a case sitting as a deputy judge of the Queen's Bench Division. This is possible because at the present time all the permanent London official referees are authorised to sit as deputy High Court judges when called upon so to do. In 1983 the Court of Appeal reaffirmed the finality of an official referee's findings of fact in these words:

"In our judgment the policy behind the rule is clear. In the ordinary way the official referee's decision on fact is to be final. He has to go into very complicated and detailed factual questions which take a great deal of time. As a matter of policy, when an official referee with his great experience of such matters, makes a decision, it should ordinarily be final."[4]

## Appeal on law

By Order 58, rule 4(1)(a) an appeal shall lie to the Court of Appeal from a decision of an official referee on a point of law or as to costs only. The expression "point of law" is widely construed and includes the exercise of a judicial discretion[5] and decisions of fact which no reasonable court could arrive at.[6] The whole of rule 4(1) is now subject to paragraph (2) providing that "in relation to any decision of an official referee referred to in paragraph (1) section 18 of the Act shall apply as if the official referee were a judge of the High Court." The reference is to section 18(1) of the Supreme Court Act 1981, and this provision has the effect of introducing the need for leave to appeal in certain cases noted below.[7] Apart from these restricted cases appeal on law lies as of right.

**14–02**

## Appeal on fact: fraud and professional negligence

After it had been held in *Osenton & Co.* v. *Johnston*[8] that the absence of a right of appeal on fact rendered professional negligence cases unsuited to be official referees' business, the law was altered and appeal now lies from a decision of fact relevant to a charge of professional negligence. No leave to appeal is needed. See also paragraph 6–05, above. Fraud has long been an exception to the ban on appeal on fact. The present rule, Order 58, rule 4(1), provides that "appeal shall lie . . . (b) from a

**14–03**

---

[4] *Moody* v. *Ellis* (1984) 26 Build.L.R. 39 at 46.
[5] Para. 14–06 below.
[6] Para. 14–07 below.
[7] Para. 14–04 below.
[8] [1942] A.C. 136.

decision of an official referee on a question of fact relevant to a charge of fraud or breach of professional duty." The words "relevant to a charge of . . . breach of professional duty" do not cover consequential issues such as those relating to quantification of damages[9] unless perhaps they form an ingredient of the cause of action.[10]

### Interlocutory appeals

**14–04**    Prior to 1977 there was doubt whether leave was needed to bring an interlocutory appeal from an official referee's interlocutory decision.[11] This doubt arose out of an apparent conflict between the provisions of Order 58, rule 4, which gave an unfettered right of appeal on law but made no mention of interlocutory appeals, and section 31 of the Supreme Court of Judicature Act 1925[12] under which leave was required to bring interlocutory appeals to the Court of Appeal from High Court judges. In *Technistudy Ltd.* v. *Kelland*[13] the Court of Appeal held that leave was not needed on an interlocutory appeal from an official referee but found that this outcome was anomalous. Roskill L.J. said[14] that the matter ought to be referred to the Rules Committee "in order that the position can be placed beyond doubt and, if it were thought right so to provide, that interlocutory appeals from an official referee can only be brought with leave." This was done, and by the Rules of the Supreme Court (Amendment No. 1) Order 1977[15] Order 58, rule 4 was amended by the insertion of paragraph (2) which now reads "In relation to any decision of an official referee referred to in paragraph (1) section 18 of the Act shall apply as if the official referee were a judge of the High Court."[16] The effect of incorporating section 18 is that on interlocutory appeals the leave is needed either of the official referee or of the Court of Appeal, unless the order is a consent order, in which case only the official referee can give leave.

### Appeal as to costs

**14–05**    This lies to the Court of Appeal by virtue of Order 58, rule 4(1)(*a*) but leave of the official referee who has made the order is required by virtue of section 18(1)(*h*) of the Supreme Court Act 1981, applied by Order 58, rule 4(2).

---

[9] *Moody* v. *Ellis* (1984) 26 Build.L.R. 39.
[10] *Leach* v. *Crossley* (1984) 30 Build.L.R. 95, *per* Lawton L.J. at 106.
[11] See *Viner* v. *Goldstein* [1946] 2 All E.R. 276.
[12] Now s.18(1) of the Supreme Court Act 1981.
[13] [1976] 1 W.L.R. 1043.
[14] *Ibid.* at 1046.
[15] S.I. 1977 No. 332.
[16] For an authoritative exposition of the position see *Giles (Electrical Engineers) Ltd.* v. *Plessey Communications Systems Ltd.* (1984) 29 Build.L.R. 21, *per* Sir John Donaldson M.R. at 21, 22.

## Exercise of discretion

In *Instrumatic Ltd.* v. *Supabrase Ltd.*[17] an official referee had in the    **14–06**
exercise of his discretion struck out a claim for want of prosecution by
reason of delay. The Court of Appeal held that they had jurisdiction to
hear an appeal from this decision. See *per* Denning M.R.[18]: "If a tribunal
exercises its discretion in a way which is plainly wrong, it errs in point
of law," and see *per* Edmund Davies L.J.[19]: "Whether there was material
justifying the court in exercising its discretion by way of dismissing an
action for want of prosecution is, in my judgment, clearly a matter of
law."

## Law and fact

Because there is no appeal on fact unsuccessful litigants are tempted    **14–07**
to argue that to draw a wrong inference from primary facts is to err in
law. The boundaries of this argument as it applies to appeals from
official referees were fully explored by the Court of Appeal in *Peak Construction (Liverpool) Ltd.* v. *McKinney Foundations Ltd.*[20] In that case Sal-
mon L.J. set out the position as follows[21]:

> "The plaintiffs contend that this finding is largely a finding of
> fact. And so it is. Since there is no appeal from an official referee on
> such a finding of fact the plaintiffs argue that the official referee's
> finding is unassailable. A finding of primary fact is as a rule
> undoubtedly unassailable. In the present case the primary facts
> which I have summarised cannot be challenged and indeed are
> undisputed. They all appear from the admitted documents. The
> proper inference to be drawn from those primary facts no doubt is
> also a question of fact. The deputy official referee has drawn the
> inference that the whole of the 58 weeks delay is attributable to the
> defendants' breach and none of it to unreasonable dilatoriness on
> the part of the corporation. This court would not be justified in
> interfering with this decision merely because it thinks that it would
> probably have come to a different conclusion. If however we are
> satisfied that the deputy official referee 'acted without any evidence
> or upon a view of the facts which could not reasonably be enter-
> tained' or if the primary facts 'not only do . . . not justify [the find-
> ing] but . . . lead irresistibly to the opposite inference or
> conclusion' this court has the power and indeed the duty to

---

[17] [1969] 1 W.L.R. 519.
[18] *Ibid.* at 521.
[19] *Ibid.* at 522.
[20] (1971) 69 L.G.R. 1; 1 Build.L.R. 114.
[21] (1971) 69 L.G.R. 1 at 8.

intervene: see *Edwards* v. *Bairstow* [1956] A.C. 14, *per* Viscount Simonds at 29."[22]

### Procedure: documents for the Court of Appeal

**14–08**    The procedure on an appeal from the official referee is the same as that on appeal from any other decision of the High Court and does not call for examination here. See Order 59 as to appeals to the Court of Appeal and note that by rule 1 thereof "This Order applies . . . to every appeal to the Court of Appeal (including so far as it is applicable thereto, any appeal to that Court from an official referee . . . )"

However one matter calls for comment as peculiarly affecting official referees' appeals. This is the question of the judge's notes of the evidence and of his judgment. When the official referees sit in the Royal Courts of Justice in London a tape recording is made of the proceedings[23] and on appeal the judgment and such parts of the evidence as may be relevant are transcribed and submitted to the Court of Appeal as in any other appeal from the High Court. But this recording (or a shorthand note) is not made when the London official referees sit outside London or in many of the places where the provincial official referees sit,[24] unless they specially request it and certify accordingly.[25] Therefore where an appeal is brought in a case not so recorded the documents to be lodged with the Court of Appeal pursuant to Order 59, rule 9 will include "(*f*) . . . the judge's note of his reasons"; and "(*g*) . . . such part of the judge's note of the evidence as are relevant to any such questions." The official referee's notes should be bespoken from the judge's clerk.[26]

---

[22] See also *per* Edmund-Davies L.J. in *Peak Construction (Liverpool) Ltd.* v. *McKinney Foundations Ltd.* 1 Build.L.R. 114 at 123.

[23] See para. 13–08 above.

[24] See para. 15–10 below.

[25] See para. 13–08 above.

[26] For the procedure see *The Supreme Court Practice 1988*, para. 59/9/3.

# Chapter 15
# Provincial Official Referees

### Origin

The Beeching Report thought that the benefit of the official referees' **15–01** services was too much confined to London. The report said:

> "We are anxious that similar facilities to those existing in London should be available at the main centres of court activity in the provinces. It is for this reason that we recommend that Circuit Administrators should regard it as one of their functions to ensure that arrangements are made for the services of official referees to be available when required. It might simplify the arrangements if each of the present three official referees assumed responsibility in this respect for two circuits."[1]

The suggestion made in the last sentence was not adopted; instead there were set up part-time provincial official referees. The Courts Act 1971, section 25, provided that official referees' business should be transacted by such circuit judges as the Lord Chancellor might determine,[2] and in addition to continuing the functions of the London official referees by appointing them to do official referees' business the Lord Chancellor also appointed circuit judges in the provinces to act as part-time official referees. In June 1972 the Lord Chancellor made a determination under section 25 of the Act[3] in respect of two named judges for each of the circuits except the South Eastern circuit, and he has since designated many other judges to transact official referees' business in the provinces.

---

[1] Report of the Royal Commission on Assizes and Quarter Sessions 1969, Cmd. 4153.
[2] Repealed by the Supreme Court Act 1981, s.152(4) and Sched. 7 with effect from January 1, 1982 and replaced by s.68 of that Act in different language—see Appendix A below.
[3] Now s.68(1) of the Supreme Court Act 1981.

### The Lord Chancellor's direction

**15–02**    Rule 5 of Order 36, dealing with the allocation of work to official referees by rota[4] would be inappropriate in the case of the provincial official referees. Subsection (4) of section 25 of the Courts Act 1971,[5] provided that "the distribution of official referees' business . . . shall be determined in accordance with directions given by or on behalf of the Lord Chancellor," and pursuant to this power the Lord Chancellor in June 1972 directed that where a reference to one of the provincial official referees was to be made the following procedure should be followed:

(1) Before the reference is made the district registrar should inquire of the courts administrator whether the particular circuit judge is likely to be available to take the reference.

(2) If he is, the reference should be made to the circuit judge by name, but this is without prejudice to the power of that judge to order the transfer of the case to the other circuit judge taking official referees' business on the same circuit or to one of the judges taking official referees' business in London if that judge consents.

(3) The district registrar should also ascertain where the circuit judge is likely to sit for the purpose of taking the business referred to him. An officer of the district registry for the town of sitting should act as the circuit judge's clerk for the purpose of Order 36, rule 6,[6] as if the business had been allocated to him under rule 5 of that Order.

With the passage of time this direction has become largely obsolete and each circuit has developed its own internal office procedure. For an example see the Northern circuit practice direction set out in part in Appendix C, paragraph C–03 below.

### Provincial litigants' option

**15–03**    The Lord Chancellor's direction of June 1972, made under his power to determine the distribution of official referees' business, also provided that the London official referees should retain their ability to take cases referred to them from district registries and to sit if desirable outside London. This overlapping of the jurisdictions was the subject of judicial scrutiny in *Durston* v. *O'Keefe*[7] where Forbes J. summarised the situation as follows:

"Notwithstanding these last appointments [*sc.* of provincial official

---

[4] See para. 7–08 above.

[5] Replaced by s.68(6) of the Supreme Court Act 1981.

[6] The reference to the official referee's clerk was deleted from Ord. 36, r. 6 as from October 1, 1982.

[7] [1974] 1 W.L.R. 775.

referees] the circuit judges taking the official referees' business in London—whom I might call the 'old' official referees—are still available to deal with such business outside London if it is referred to them ... A choice is thus open to the district registrar who desires to transfer a cause to a circuit judge discharging the functions of an official referee. He can either transfer it to the London circuit judges discharging these functions (when the judge dealing with it may sit either in London or outside) or to one of the circuit judges appointed to discharge these functions on the appropriate circuit."[8]

Whether any given case will be remitted to the local or to the London official referees will depend upon the wishes of the parties and the weight of the case. If the parties are agreed, the District Registrar will be unlikely to override their wishes. Otherwise, a case is unlikely to be sent to London unless either it is a more convenient forum from the viewpoint of witnesses' attendance, or the hearing is likely to last a long time. Pressure of their other work renders it undesirable for the provincial judges in some instances to take on one of the construction disputes whose length can be assessed in months rather than in weeks. The practical effect of the overlapping of the London and the provincial official referees is that, unlike those on the south-eastern circuit, provincial litigants on other circuits have the option of going by rota before one of the London official referees or of going before their local or district official referee.

### District official referees

Since 1972 the system of provincial official referees has gradually developed. Additional circuit judges have been designated to transact official referees' business according to need. All the designated judges have been attached to the major courts administrators' groups on their circuits and there are thus official referees, now ordinarily referred to as district official referees, available in all large centres and attached to each courts administrators' group. The district official referees are part-time official referees, dealing with other circuit judges' work when not called upon to do official referees' business.[9] Cases are assigned on a geographical basis to the district official referee for the area concerned, unless trial elsewhere is asked for on a summons to remit or a summons for directions and the work of the provincial official referees has steadily increased.[10]

**15–04**

---

[8] *Ibid.* at 777.
[9] In Liverpool a local direction provides for county court cases in classes akin to official referees' business to be heard by the district official referee.
[10] The number of cases brought in to the provincial official referees in 1987 is unofficially estimated at 584.

### Initial procedure

**15–05**   Where a writ marked "official referees' business" is issued out of a provincial district registry other than on the south-eastern circuit, it will be allocated to the district official referee for the area in which the district registry is situated. If a hearing in another area is required it will probably be better to leave the writ unmarked and to apply subsequently to the District Registrar to transfer the case to the desired area. Where a writ is marked "official referees' business" the District Registrar has no jurisdiction over it and all applications have to be made to the judge.[11] Similarly, where it is desired to start an action in a district registry (other than on the south-eastern circuit) but to bring it before a London official referee either in London or elsewhere, it will be advisable not to mark the writ but to apply after notice of intention to defend to the District Registrar to transfer the case to the London official referees. If the writ were marked "official referees' business" the only way of securing the services of the London official referees would be by applying to the district official referee for transfer under Order 36, rule 7, in which event the consent of the transferee is needed. Where the writ is not marked "official referees' business" an application for transfer may be made to the District Registrar in whose registry it was issued; the District Registrar will inquire where the parties wish the case to be heard and if he grants the order he will assign the case to the district official referee for the area concerned. On the Northern Circuit the procedure has been formalised in a practice direction, part of which is set out at Appendix C below paragraph C–03.

### Summons for directions

**15–06**   Pursuant to paragraph (c) of the Lord Chancellor's directions an officer of the district registry takes the place of the London official referee's clerk. Inquiries and applications for summonses should be addressed either to the Chief Clerk or to "the Clerk to the Official Referee" at the relevant registry, who will upon application arrange a hearing of the summons for directions. The judges familiarise themselves with the case before hearing the summons and while it is desirable if possible to dispose of interlocutory matters at a single sitting, it is generally found that a second or adjourned hearing is necessary in order to secure that all proper steps have been taken before a hearing date is fixed. An interesting development found on the north-eastern circuit is the postal order for directions: "What normally happens, because of distances involved and convenience and cost to parties, is that the judge reads the file immediately after it is assigned to him and indicates what directions he thinks are likely to be necessary. The clerk writes to the parties

---

[11] *Cf. Durston* v. *O'Keefe* [1974] 1 W.L.R. 775 and para. 7–06 above.

104

advising them of this view and telling them that the judge is willing to deal with the directions by correspondence if they are agreed. If there is some area of disagreement then a date is fixed for the hearing of all or part of the directions. Many cases proceed to hearing without a prior personal attendance before the district official referee."[12] On the northern circuit also the district official referees are willing to deal with agreed orders by correspondence where the cases come from outlying districts. While Order 36, rule 6 requires an application for directions to be made it does not require the official referee to hear the parties *viva voce* and in the simpler non-controversial cases this procedure would appear to be apt and to effect a considerable saving of costs.

## Procedure generally

The procedure as to allocation of the judge is the only respect in which interlocutory procedure in the provinces differs from that in London. The provisions of Order 36, other than rule 5(3) as to the rota, apply equally to all official referee cases and the preceding chapters should be consulted upon procedure generally.[12a]

**15–07**

## Venue

The provincial official referees may be asked to sit at any place convenient to the parties provided that a suitable courtroom can be made available and that it is within the boundaries of the circuit to which they have been assigned. In practice the circuits have found that the larger centres are the most practicable. Thus on the Wales and Chester circuit northern cases are ordinarily heard at Mold or Chester and southern cases at Cardiff. On the western circuit three judges operate respectively from the court centres at Bristol, Exeter and Winchester. On the northern circuit judges are based at Liverpool and Manchester respectively and on the north-eastern circuit the judges are respectively attached to the three courts administrators' groups, at Leeds, Newcastle-on-Tyne, and Sheffield. On the Midland circuit judges sit at Stafford, Birmingham and Nottingham. The system is administered with a great deal of flexibility and arrangements may vary from time to time; the local courts administrator's office should be consulted as to the up-to-date position and practice. An example of flexibility is that for example in a case originating in Carlisle the official referee may hear the summons for directions at Liverpool but if the case calls for local trial, he will arrange to sit at Carlisle for the hearing. The busiest circuit appears to be the northern, where in 1987 85 cases were set down at Liverpool

**15–08**

---

[12] *Ex rel.* Courts Administrator, North-Eastern Circuit.
[12a] For a full account of procedure by a provincial referee, see "Official Referees' Business in the Provinces" by Judge T. R. Heald, (1987) 53 Arbitration 232.

and 77 at Manchester; both these centres have court rooms set aside for official referees' cases.

### Transfer

**15–09**    Another aspect of flexibility is transfer between judges, pursuant to Order 36, rule 7. This may take place between judges on the same circuit, where the assigned judge is indisposed or unavailable owing to other work, and also between London and provincial judges. If a relatively small provincial case finds its way into the London list the London judge may ask the local judge to take it over. Conversely there have been cases where a long provincial case has been transferred to London. Those applications which the trial judge is not allowed to hear[13] should, by arrangement with the judge's clerk, be transferred to be heard by another official referee on the same circuit.

### Hearing

**15–10**    Fixed dates are ordinarily given for the trial of official referees' business by district official referees. Because these judges are part-time official referees and have their other judicial business to attend to it is important that a realistic estimate be given of the length of the case. For the same reason it is essential to notify the judge's clerk at once if the case is settled. For preparation for trial, trial and appeal, see Chapters 12, 13 and 14 above. Some centres have regular times set aside for official referees' business. Thus at Nottingham three one-month periods per year are set aside for hearings and one day per month for summonses. One matter which provincial litigants should especially address their minds to is the question of the shorthand note. In most provincial centres a shorthand note is not taken unless application is made to the judge to certify[14] or the parties make their own arrangements, with the judge's approval. However in some centres, for example Cardiff and Newcastle upon Tyne, a note or tape recording is taken as a matter of course, either of the judgment or of the whole case, and litigants are advised to asertain what the local practice is.

---

[13] See para. 8–09 above.
[14] See para. 13–08 above.

106

# Chapter 16
# The Official Referees' Users' Committee

### Formation and composition

This valuable committee was formed in 1982 and held its first meeting    **16–01**
on January 12, 1983. Its Chairman is the senior official referee and its
members comprise the permanent London official referees together
with representatives of the following bodies:

(1)  The Chartered Institute of Arbitrators;
(2)  The Royal Institute of British Architects;
(3)  The Royal Institution of Chartered Surveyors;
(4)  The Institution of Civil Engineers;
(5)  The Association of Consulting Engineers;
(6)  The Federation of Master Builders;
(7)  The National Building Employers Confederation;
(8)  The Federation of Civil Engineering Contractors;
(9)  The National Housebuilding Council;
(10  The Association of Metropolitan Authorities;
(11)  The Association of District Authorities;
(12)  The Bar Council;
(13)  The Official Referees Bar Association;
(14)  The Law Society;
(15)  The Barristers Clerks Association.

In 1987 the following bodies were added:

(16)  The Department of the Environment Construction Industry
     Directorate;
(17)  The Institution of Civil Engineers;
(18)  The British Insurance Association;
(19)  The Confederation of Associations of Specialist Sub-Contrac-
     tors;

107

(20) The Confederation of Associations of Specialised Engineering Contractors.

The Secretary to the Committee is the Clerk to the Senior official referee, Mr. Richard Carter, and members of the official referees' staff also attend meetings.

## Objectives

16–02    The Committee's objects are formally stated to be "to ensure that the official referees' courts meet the needs of the construction industry and of others who resort to them and that the courts should have the means with which to meet those needs."[1] The Committee monitors the work of the courts and provides a forum "in which any dissatisfaction felt by users can be readily brought to the attention of the official referees and of their staff."[2] The Committee is also concerned with improvements in law and procedure and makes representations to the appropriate bodies when changes are considered desirable. The Committee meets whenever necessary and in addition to its formal functions it provides a valuable meeting point for the exchange of ideas between the different disciplines concerned with the work of the official referees' courts.

## Work of the Committee

16–03    It is no coincidence that the formation of the Committee was followed in 1984 by the ventilation in the House of Commons of the complaints about delays in the official referees' courts referred to in paragraph 4–08, above and the Committee may justly claim a share in the credit for the increase in the numbers of official referees which ensued, and the consequent reduction in the delays. Similarly their support for the campaign for improved accommodation played its part in the successful outcome whereby the court is moving to superior accommodation of its own. The Committee has also made successful representations to the Lord Chancellor's Department which led to the 1986 changes in the rules about expert evidence.[3] Further proposals by the Committee for amendments in the Rules of the Supreme Court are understood to be under consideration. The Committee has also considered the effects of the decision in *Northern Regional Health Authority* v. *Crouch Construction Ltd*,[4] a decision by which they say they "were dismayed"[5]: and they have made successful representations about the reporting of official referees' decisions.[6] They have in a short time become the recog-

---

[1] First Report of Official Referees Users' Committee, para. 2.1.
[2] *Ibid.* para. 2.2.
[3] See paras. 9–02 and 9–03 above.
[4] [1984] 1 Q.B. 644; see para. 6–08 above.
[5] First Report of Committee, para. 5.1.
[6] See para. 13–10 above.

nised channel through which proposals for improvements of all kinds, whether originating with the court or with its users, are promoted.

## Reports

The Committee's first report was issued in 1987 and it is the intention **16–04** to issue future reports annually. The first report was brought to the attention of Parliament on March 18, 1987 when in the House of Lords Lord Broxbourne asked the Government "whether consideration has yet been given to the recent report of the official referees' Users' Committee and whether action is yet in hand to effect the recommended improvements."[7] The Lord Chancellor (Lord Hailsham of St. Marylebone) replied that action was being taken to secure improved accommodation for the court and the adequate reporting of its decisions. Further amendments to the Rules of the Supreme Court were under consideration, but no decision had yet been taken on matters requiring legislation. Lord Silkin of Dulwich referred to the case of *Crouch*, "the effect of which is thought to be that multiplicity of proceedings is encouraged where it need not be," but the Lord Chancellor thought that the questions raised by *Crouch* required "rather careful and wider consultation than it has yet received."[8]

A second report was issued in May 1988, covering the Committee's activities from January 1987 to April 1988.

## Representations

The Committee is always ready to consider suggestions or com- **16–05** plaints. Communications should be addressed to the Secretary, the Official Referees' Users' Committee. The address at the time of writing is Royal Courts of Justice, Strand, London WC2A 2LL, but as from the move to new premises it will be St. Dunstan's House, Fetter Lane, London EC4.

---

[7] *Hansard*, H.L., vol. 485, col. 1417.
[8] *Ibid.* col. 1418.

# Part III
# Miscellaneous Jurisdictions

# Chapter 17
# Taking Accounts

## History

The taking of accounts was one of the earliest duties of official refer-  **17–01**
ees and during the first two decades of their existence it formed a substantial part of their work. As has been noted[1] provision had been made
even before the setting up of official referees for the reference of
"matters of mere account," and one of the matters singled out by section 57 of the Judicature Act 1873, for trial by the new official referees
was "any question of account." When by section 14 of the Arbitration
Act 1889, the new jurisdiction was re-stated, the matters referrable
included those where "the question in dispute consists wholly or in
part of matters of account." The specific reference to accounts disappeared when, following the report of the Evershed Committee, the
enabling formula, now transferred from statute to the Rules of
the Supreme Court, was simplified.[2] But it re-emerged in 1982 when the
formula was reintroduced to the Rules by way of a definition of "official
referees' business"; that definition includes a cause or matter "which
involves a prolonged examination of . . . accounts."[3]

## Former practice

The obsolescent procedure of reference for inquiry and report was  **17–02**
formerly used for the taking of accounts. The case was tried by a judge
of the Queen's Bench or Chancery Division and if accounts were called
for the taking of the account was referred for inquiry and report.[4] This
procedure is still available if any litigant or court wishes to employ it

---

[1] See para. 2–03 above.
[2] See para. 4–04 above.
[3] Ord. 36, r. 1(2)(a).
[4] Other issues were jealously retained by the Division: see *Hurlbatt* v. *Barrett & Co.* [1893]
1 Q.B. 77.

and is described in Chapter 19 below.[5] What is used today on the rare occasions when taking an account is remitted to the official referee separated from other matters tried in the same case, is the procedure by way of remitting "a question or issue of fact" for trial.[6]

### Official referees' procedure

**17–03**　It was early decided that the method of taking accounts in Chancery chambers need not be followed by official referees. The case of *Re Taylor, Turpin* v. *Pain*[7] which decided this point, is still today a valuable guide to the taking of accounts in the official referees' courts. It was an inquiry-and-report case, but the procedure followed as described in the judgment is equally applicable to the taking of accounts by way of trial of an issue. What happened in that case was that a widow by her will directed her executors and trustees to carry on her farming business; beneficiaries claimed an account and the taking of this account was referred to an official referee. His report was attacked as being insufficiently detailed and it was alleged to be defective because the official referee had not followed the practice in Chancery chambers. Chitty J. decided that the account had been properly taken. He said:

> "I am asked to remit this report, with directions that these accounts be taken and vouched in the way usually adopted before a Chief Clerk . . . The official referee could not take the accounts in that way; an attempt was made to do so in chambers, which failed. The official referee in my judgment is not bound to take accounts referred to him in the same way as the Chancery clerks do.[8]
>
> There is an advantage in some instances in taking the accounts before the official referee according to the existing practice. The official referee does not proceed by affidavit and then by cross-examination; what he can do and what he has done in this case is, to have the witnesses before him, and the accounts, and also the account books, and then to sit continuously, as he did in this case, till the matter is finished. The parties come before him and give their evidence *viva voce*, certain accounts are produced, and evidence is taken there and then upon the matter, and there is cross-examination of course if need be; the referee has seen the witnesses and has made notes . . . this method of taking accounts no doubt is

---

[5] For an example, see the leading case of *London Chatham & Dover Ry.* v. *S. E. Ry.* [1893] A.C. 429 (official referee held to have wrongly added interest to the account). The report should state the items allowed and disallowed: *Dunkirk Colliery Co.* v. *Lever* (1878) 9 Ch.D. 20 at 28.
[6] Ord. 36, r. 3(2).
[7] (1890) 44 Ch.D. 128.
[8] *Ibid.* at 136.

not so formal or so rigid as is the manner of taking accounts in the Chancery Division."[9]

Chancery accounts are still governed by Order 43 of the Rules of the Supreme Court, but the procedure there laid down is not followed by the official referees, whose procedure as exemplified in *Re Taylor* seems to have been thought superior to the Chancery practice: see *Rochefoucauld* v. *Boustead*.[10]

### Present day practice

The taking of an account in isolation is today a rare event. If however **17–04** an order is made transferring an accounts issue to the official referee it is the duty of the plaintiff or failing him the defendant to make an application for directions pursuant to Order 36, rule 6. In London the matter is then allocated to one of the referees in rotation. But ordinarily the accounting process forms part of the trial of an action which involves other issues as well as the quantum of the debt. In such instances the official referee may decide to try the substantive issues of fact and take the account later, or he may do both together, according to the balance of convenience. In either event in giving directions the official referee will be helped by; and indeed may require, a document in Scott Schedule form setting out the case of the respective parties on each item. In cases where the plaintiff does not know the facts the drafting of this schedule will have to be postponed until after discovery. Thus in the not uncommon case where a commission agent who has left his employer's service claims commission on repeat orders, full discovery will be ordered and after the plaintiff has ascertained what he can from inspection and otherwise he will be required to serve an account in Scott Schedule form and the defendant will be ordered to plead to it.[11] Discovery is of obvious importance in cases where the defendant is an accounting party, and interrogatories as well as lists of documents may be called for.

### Trial

When an accounting issue comes to trial the matter is dealt with by **17–05** *viva voce* evidence on each of the disputed items and by cross-examination very much in the way described by Chitty J. in *Re Taylor*.[12] Where the dispute arises out of discrepancies between the books of account of

---

[9] *Ibid.* at 137.
[10] [1897] 1 Ch. 196. The headnote reads "A very difficult account directed to be taken by an official referee instead of in chambers on account of the great saving of time which would thus be effected."
[11] On Scott Schedules generally see Chap. 8 above.
[12] See para. 17–03 above.

the respective parties the expert evidence of accountants may be called for. As to experts reports and the appointment of a court expert, see Chapter 9 above. The trial of the issue is conducted in public in the same manner as any other trial in the official referees' courts.[13]

---

[13] On trial generally see Chap. 13 above. For the distinction between an action for a specified sum and an action for an account see *Re Wells dec'd.* [1962] 1 W.L.R. 397.

# Chapter 18
# Assessing Damages

## Jurisdiction

Where a judgment has been signed for damages to be assessed that **18–01** assessment is ordinarily made by a Master pursuant to Order 37, rule 1. But by rule 4(1) of that Order the court may "order that the assessment of the damages shall be referred to an official referee . . . " Where an order is made under rule 4(1)(*a*) the assessment becomes official referees' business by virtue of the provisions of section 68(6) of the Supreme Court Act 1981,[1] and of rule 1(1) of Order 36 whereby "the other provisions of these rules" apply to official referees' business "subject to the provisions of this Order." Transfer of the assessment of damages to the official referees is a frequent occurrence in modern practice. The judgments leading to such assessments are usually judgments in default of notice of intention to defend pursuant to Order 13, rule 2 or in default of defence pursuant to Order 19, rule 3, but sometimes a court giving judgment on the merits after a trial will remit the quantification of the damages to an official referee. A judgment for the value of goods to be assessed falls within the same procedure.[2]

## What cases remitted

Whether a case is suitable for remission to the official referees for the **18–02** assessment of damages depends upon whether it is considered to be "official referees' business" as defined in Order 36, rule 1(2)[3] and is judged in the same way as transfer for trial, discussed in full at paragraphs 6–02 to 6–06, above. Thus the assessment of damages for personal injuries will not be trransferred but the assessment of damages in a building or engineering case is a fit subject for transfer. Assessments involving, in the words of Order 36, rule 1(2)(*a*) "a prolonged

---

[1] See Appendix A below, para. A–02.
[2] Ord. 37, r. 5.
[3] See para. 1–05 above.

examination of accounts" are clear candidates for this treatment and a class of case frequently so dealt with is the dilapidations claim, where a defendant, while admitting that dilapidations exist, nevertheless disputes the plaintiff's particulars and alleged costs of repair. These are pre-eminently Scott Schedule cases.

### Procedure

**18–03**    The order referring the assessment of damages to an official referee is made by "the court"[4] that is, by the judge after a trial or in a default case by application to the Master. Once remitted, the provisions of Order 36 apply and the procedure laid down in that order must therefore be followed. An application for directions has to be made, although whether this must be done within the 14 days limited by rule 6(1) is perhaps doubtful. It was clear enough that this applied under the wording of rule 6(1) and (2) before the amendments of October 1982 but by those amendments the requirement is tied to "the date of the order transferring the cause or matter" and this may be thought to be now limited to transfer under the new rule 3 and to exclude a reference under Order 37. However that may be, the official referees may be expected to continue their practice of requiring a summons for directions to be taken out in assessment cases, and in practice a claimant must do so otherwise he will not get a hearing date assigned. Upon the summons being applied for the case will be allocated in London to one of the permanent official referees in rotation, or in the provinces to the district official referee.[5] The case then remains in the list of the assigned judge, who will deal with all interlocutory applications and will try the case, unless some reason arises for transfer to another judge.[6]

### Directions

**18–04**    In an assessment case all the ordinary directions may be given save that *ex hypothesi* no question relating to liability may be raised. A plaintiff may however be called upon to amplify his particulars of damage and a defendant may be called upon to plead to them. In many cases a Scott Schedule will be ordered.[7] Parties who intend to call valuers or accountants as witnesses must bear in mind that these are experts in respect of whose evidence leave must be obtained and that experts' reports must be disclosed prior to the hearing.[8] A fixed date for the hearing will ordinarily be ordered.

---

[4] Ord. 37, r. 4.
[5] See paras. 7–08 and 15–06 above.
[6] See para. 7–12 above.
[7] See generally Chap. 10 above.
[8] See generally Chap. 9 above.

## Hearing

The assessment of damages is arrived at in open court after a trial **18–05** similar in all respects to the trial of an issue as to quantum. The official referee will assume that the contents of the statement of claim upon which judgment has been given are accurate, save as regards the damages alleged. Judgment is given in open court and the finding and any order for costs is embodied in the certificate drawn up by the judge's clerk and signed by the official referee, after which the certified amount is entered on the form of judgment already obtained.

# Chapter 19
# Inquiry and Report

### An obsolescent procedure

**19–01**   The holding of an inquiry into facts and the making of a report thereon to the court was one of the original duties laid upon official referees at their inception in 1873[1] and reproduced in statutory form a process that had already grown up to relieve the courts of decisions of fact for which jury trial was unsuitable.[2] The jursidiction was first embodied in section 56 of the Judicature Act 1873[3] and has been re-enacted in substantially the same form from time to time until the present day, when it is reproduced in section 68(2)(*b*) of the Supreme Court Act 1981[4] and by Order 36, rule 8 of the Rules of the Supreme Court.[5] However after 1884 and 1889, when official referees were given the power to try the whole of a case[6] the procedure by way of trial proved itself so superior to the procedure by way of inquiry and report that as the years went by less and less use was made of the older procedure. By 1895 use of inquiry and report had so declined that in that year 16 cases were referred for inquiry and report as against 195 for trial.[7] It continued however to be used sparingly from time to time until recent years. By 1914 the number referred had dwindled to three, and between 1964 and 1969 only three actions were so referred. Since 1969 one or two cases have been remitted, it seems by inadvertance, but when the disadvantages of the procedure have been pointed out to the parties they have obtained a variation of the order to remit, and have proceeded to trial. No inquiry has in fact been held since 1969. However the procedure cannot be said to be obsolete; it is there to be used if litigants discern any advantage in using it, and it must therefore be dealt with in

---

[1] See para. 2–05 above.
[2] See para. 2–03 above.
[3] See para. 2–06 above.
[4] Appendix A below.
[5] Appendix B below.
[6] See para. 3–07 above.
[7] Judicial Statistics 1895.

this work. And if effect is ever given to the suggestion made by Donald-son M.R. in *Crouch*[8] that official referees be given the power to sub-refer the "nuts and bolts" of a suit to an arbitrator for inquiry and report, the decisions mentioned in this chapter will become relevant.

### Application: "issue arising"

The procedure as now embodied in Order 36, rule 8, provides for the **19–02** reference for inquiry and report of "any question or issue of fact arising therein"—namely in any cause or matter in the Chancery or Queen's Bench Divisions. It has been held that only issues which must arise and not merely those which may arise may be so transferred. This was decided in *Weed* v. *Ward*[9] under the original provision contained in section 56 of the Judicature Act 1873. The phrase in that section was "any question arising in any cause or matter" and was thus substantially the same as that contained in the present rule. The Court of Appeal (Cotton, Lindley and Lopes L.JJ.) held that "any question arising" meant any question which must necessarily arise. In that case the plaintiff had alleged a representation by the defendant as to the profits of a business under such circumstances that if the statement were not true the plain-tiff would be entitled to damages and rescission. North J. had referred for inquiry and report the question of what was the amount of the said profits. This was a point which might or might not arise at the trial of the action. Cotton L.J. said[10]:

> "Counsel contends that the section only authorises a reference to an issue which must in any event be decided in the action. For instance if the plaintiff sues in respect of the obstruction of light and air then unless the defendant sets up some case which would preclude the plaintiff from complaining of an obstruction of light and air, the question whether the light has been really obstructed must necessarily be decided in the action, and it might under certain circumstances be desirable that a reference of the question whether it has been obstructed should be ordered in order that a report might be made to the judge to enable him better to decide that question. I see no reason to doubt that such an order may be made at any stage in the action, if the question is one which must necessarily arise and must certainly be decided. If indeed it was alleged by the defendant that supposing he may have obstructed the light the terms of an agreement which had been entered into by the plaintiff prevent the plaintiff from raising the question, then I would say that the question whether there was an agreement

---

[8] [1984] Q.B. 644 at 675; passage reproduced at para. 6–09 above.
[9] (1899) 40 Ch.D. 555, distinguished in *Hurlbatt* v. *Barrett* [1893] 1 Q.B. 77, a case on account. See para. 17–02 above.
[10] *Weed* v. *Ward* (1899) Ch.D. 555 at 560.

having the effect contended for ought to be decided first . . . I think the proper construction of [section 56] is that suggested by counsel, that it only refers to issues which must necessarily arise in the action and not to issues which will not arise unless the plaintiff is successful on other issues."

The appeal was allowed: Lopes L.J. said that under any wider interpretation the section might be made "an instrument of torture to litigants and might be used for the purpose of obtaining from them information to which the party obtaining it had no right."[11] This strict rule does not apply to the taking of accounts, which are governed by different statutory provisions.[12]

### Cases fit for inquiry and report

**19–03**    Presumably any case thought fit for the procedure by way of trial of the whole case or of an issue arising therein[13] would be considered apt for inquiry and report. Reported cases of remission for inquiry and report include: action for injunction to restrain nuisance by noise[14]; agency[15]; account[16]; assessment of damages[17]; and a case involving services rendered, an unpaid bill of exchange and fraudulent misrepresentation.[18]

### Procedure

**19–04**    Application is made by summons to the Master asking for an order referring to the official referee for inquiry and report "any question or issue of fact" arising in any cause or matter in the Chancery Division or Queen's Bench Division, subject however to any right to trial by jury.[19] When the order is made the further consideration of the case by the parent division stands adjourned unless the court otherwise orders.[20] The case is rota'd and entered in the same way as cases referred for trial.[21] Application for directions should be made by the plaintiff within 14 days after the order transferring the reference. Upon default in this regard any other party may himself apply for directions or may apply to have the matter returned to the remitting court.[22] An oddity of the rule

[11] *Ibid.* at 562.
[12] See para. 17–04 above.
[13] See para. 6–03 above.
[14] *Larkin* v. *Lloyd* (1891) 64 L.T. 507.
[15] *Burrard* v. *Callisher* (1882) 30 W.R. 321.
[16] *Re Taylor* (1890) 44 Ch.D. 128; *Walker* v. *Burrhill* (1883) 22 Ch.D. 722.
[17] *Dunkirk Colliery Co.* v. *Lever* (1898) 9 Ch.D. 20.
[18] *Miller* v. *Pilling* (1882) 9 Q.B.D. 736.
[19] Ord. 36, r. 8, Appendix B, para. B–09 below.
[20] *Ibid.*
[21] See para. 7–09 above.
[22] Ord. 36, r. 6(2).

is that where a party applies to have the matter returned to the remitting court under Order 36, rule 6(2)(*b*) the official referee has no power (as he has in references for trial) to deal with the application as if it were a summons for directions: this power, conferred by Order 36, rule 6(3) applies to applications under rule 6(2)(*a*) but not to those under rule 6(2)(*b*). The rest of the interlocutory procedure follows the same course as in remission for trial.[23] The hearing however is different. It appears from the older reports that it used to take place in private and as the official referee is conducting an inquiry and not a trial he may presumably elect to sit as in chambers, unrobed. Because it is not a trial no shorthand note or mechanical recording is required to be taken.[24] However in the last such case to have been heard, in 1969, the hearing was in open court with robes worn.[25] The conduct of the hearing will follow the familiar pattern of opening by counsel, witnesses being examined and cross-examined, and closing speeches, but there is no judgment.[26]

## The report

Instead of delivering a judgment the official referee writes a report **19–05** which is addressed to and delivered to the court or judge by whom the matter was referred.[27] The rules require "notice thereof" to be served on the parties to the reference and in practice they are furnished with copies of the report. This document is a report on facts and not on law and is in no way comparable with a judgment. It need not give reasons for the findings of fact unless the court orders the official referee so to do.[28] But Order 36, rule 9(2) provides that the official referee may in his report submit any question arising therein for the decision of the court or make a special statement of facts from which the court may draw such inferences as it thinks fit. The nature of the proceedings and of the report was examined at length by the Queen's Bench Division in 1887 in *Baroness Wenlock* v. *River De Company*[29] where Lord Esher M.R. said:

> "The difference in my opinion between the reference contemplated by section 56 and that contemplated by section 57 is that in the one case the court may adopt or partially adopt or reject the report of the referee, as they think right, but in the other case the report has the effect of the verdict of a jury and can only be set aside in the same way or on the same grounds as a verdict of a jury can be set aside.

[23] Chap. 8 above.
[24] Ord. 68, r. 7, and see para. 13–08 above.
[25] *Ex rel.* the late Sir Walker Carter, Q.C.
[26] See *Attorney-General* v. *Birmingham Tame and Rea District Drainage Board* [1912] A.C. 788.
[27] Ord. 36, r. 9(1).
[28] See *Dunkirk Colliery Co.* v. *Lever* (1878) 9 Ch.D. 20 at 28.
[29] (1887) 19 Q.B.D. 155.

The reference under section 56 is to be for inquiry and report. It does not appear to me that the word 'inquiry' only includes an inquiry which the referee is to make with his own eyes. The word 'inquiry' in my opinion signifies an inquiry in which he is to take evidence and hold a judicial inquiry in the usual way in which such inquiries are held. The word 'inquiry' is used because it is not meant to have the same result as a trial."[30]

### Action upon the report

**19–06**     In contrast with the ordinary procedure whereby the official referee decides cases and issues with finality, subject only to a limited right of appeal, this procedure involves a further stage of consideration by the remitting court. It is provided by Order 36, rule 9(3) that upon receipt of the report the court may (a) adopt the report in whole or in part; (b) vary the report; (c) require an explanation from the official referee; (d) remit the whole or any part of the question or issue originally referred to him for further consideration by him or any other official referee; or, (e) decide the question or issue originally referred to him on the evidence taken before him, either with or without additional evidence. After argument upon the report the court will thus either send the report back to the official referee or some other official referee or will adopt it as submitted or as varied. If sent back there will be yet another hearing when the further or amended report is made, and at the end of the day the report will be adopted as settling the issues of fact with which it is concerned. Unless it is otherwise ordered it is only then that the remitting court can go on to hear argument on law, if such arises, and to enter judgment. Some slight amelioration of the time-consuming complexity of this process is discernible in the provision in Order 36, rule 8 that the consideration of the matter by the remitting court is only adjourned "unless the court otherwise orders," and the ensuing provision in Order 36, rule 9(5) that "where on a reference under rule 8 the court orders that the further consideration of the cause or matter in question shall not stand adjourned until the receipt of the official referee's report, the order may contain directions with respect to the proceedings on the receipt of the report. . . . "

### Procedure after report

**19–07**     The application to the remitting court to consider the report is made by notice of motion. And "when the report of the official referee has been made, an application to vary the report or remit the whole or any part of the question or issue originally referred may be made on the hearing by the court of the further consideration of the cause or matter,

[30] *Ibid.* at 158.

124

after giving not less than 4 days' notice thereof, and any other application with respect to the report may be made on that hearing without notice."[31]

## Merits of the procedure

At the present day the procedure presents few merits. It involves at the minimum an extra hearing as compared with the trial procedure, and may involve further costs still if the remitting court does not accept the report and requires further evidence or remission. The extra time and cost involved is clearly responsible for its decline into desuetude. However one can see that it might offer a useful procedure if some technical question arose in the course of a case in the Chancery or Queen's Bench Divisions and if the parties wished to preserve their right of appeal on fact. If the matter were remitted as the trial of an issue in the ordinary way there would be no right of appeal from the official referee's findings of fact (unless they involved fraud or professional negligence) whereas the report procedure would lead to a finding by the remitting court from which appeal on fact would lie.

**19–08**

[31] Ord. 36, r. 9(4).

# Chapter 20
# Arbitration

### Official referees as arbitrators

**20–01**    Official referees possess a jurisdiction as arbitrators entirely separate from their jurisdiction to try cases or issues in the Queen's Bench and Chancery Divisions. Since the Arbitration Act of 1889 they have been under a statutory duty to act as arbitrators in ordinary arbitrations whenever called upon by the parties so to do. Thus the official referees' court anticipated by 81 years the institution of judge-arbitrators under the Administration of Justice Act 1970, whereby judges of the Commercial Court may be nominated to conduct arbitrations. The official referees' jurisdiction, first appearing in section 11 of the Supreme Court of Judicature Act 1884, re-enacted in section 3 of the 1889 Act, now derives from section 11 of the Arbitration Act 1950, which reads as follows:

> "Where an arbitration agreement provides that the reference shall be to an official referee, any referee to whom application is made shall, subject to any order of the High Court or a judge thereof as to transfer or otherwise, hear and determine the matters agreed to be referred."

The terms of the section appear to apply only to the appointment of one official referee as a sole arbitrator. Agreements providing for hearing by two arbitrators, or by two arbitrators and an umpire are, it seems, not catered for.

### Application of Order 36 to arbitrations

**20–02**    There is some ambiguity in the application to arbitrations of the statutory provisions as to procedure. Section 68 of the Supreme Court Act 1981, clearly provides that the reference to an official referee in section 11 of the Arbitration Act 1950, shall be to a circuit judge nominated to deal with official referees' business: "(7) any reference to an official referee in any enactment, whenever passed, . . . shall unless the context otherwise requires, be construed as . . . a reference to a circuit judge nominated under subsection (1)(a)."[1] Yet the nominated judges are nominated under subsection (1)(a) to exercise the jurisdiction of the High Court, and by subsection (6) official referees' business is defined as "the cases in which the jurisdiction of the High Court may be exercised by a circuit judge nominated" etc. Moreover by Order 36, rule 1 "This Order applies to official referees' business in the Chancery Division or the Queen's Bench Division." Thus although the official referees are the persons required by section 11 of the Arbitration Act 1950, to act as arbitrators, when they do so act they are not on the face of it conducting referees' business—unless, that is, it can be maintained that arbitration under section 11 is part of "the jurisdiction of the High Court." Nevertheless, and despite the apparent limitation to High Court work in rule 1(1), other provisions of Order 36 are in terms applied to arbitration. Thus by Order 36, rule 5(2):

> "Any application under section 11 of the Arbitration Act 1950, to an official referee shall be made to the referee to whom the reference has been allocated under paragraph (3) or any other official referee to whom the reference has been transferred under the following provisions of this Order."

And the paragraph (3) thus referred to reads: "Official referees' business in the Royal Courts of Justice shall be allocated by the rota clerk to official referees in rotation." The Rules thus contemplate that arbitration is "official referees' business." Perhaps the mention in section 11 of the references being subject to an order of the High Court is sufficient to make such proceedings part of the "jurisdiction of the High Court" within subsections (1) and (6) of the Supreme Court Act 1981. However despite these difficulties rule 5 exists and there can be no doubt that the official referees will continue to apply it in the future as they have in the past.

### Entry on the rota

Where the parties have agreed either by the arbitration clause in their contract or by an ad hoc agreement in writing that their disputes shall be referred to an official referee the practice is that they should produce the contract or agreement to the rota clerk: Order 36, rule 5(2) and (3) cited above. They may not, as was formerly the case, select their official referee.[2] As with litigation, the rota clerk is required to allocate the business to the official referees in strict rotation.[3] The hearing fee, at present £30, must be paid before entry upon the rota as in the case of

**20–03**

---

[1] For subs. (1)(a) see Appendix A, below.
[2] cf. para. 4–05, above, n. 16.
[3] Ord. 36, r. 5(1).

litigation.[4] Proceedings thereafter, with one practical exception, follow the same course as in any other arbitration and the provisions of the Arbitration Acts as to hearing and award will apply. The provisions as to appeal also apply but as regards construction industry appeals are subject to the new procedure outlined in paragraph 20–08 below.[5] The parties however do not have to provide a room or hall in which the hearing will be held; the official referee will hear the matter in his own court in London or in a court in the country for which arrangements will be made by his clerk. No charge is made by the Lord Chancellor's Department beyond the initial fee of £30. The hearing is in private and robes are not worn. Nor is there any restriction on rights of audience.

### Interlocutory proceedings

20–04    The practical exception referred to above is that interlocutory proceedings follow the same procedure as in litigation. In place of the preliminary meeting of the ordinary arbitration the parties to an arbitration before an official referee are expected to ask for and submit to directions. Until October 1982 arbitration proceedings were expressly included in Order 36, rule 6, as to directions. In the amendments made by the Rules of the Supreme Court (Amendment No. 2) Order 1982,[6] the reference to an arbitration agreement was dropped from rule 6 and this part of the procedure cannot now be said to be statutory. However it is thought that the official referees will continue to follow their ordinary procedure and to deal with arbitration interlocutory proceedings in the same way as they do with litigation; for this procedure see Chapters 7 and 10, above. This procedure—summons for directions followed by an order which has to be drawn up by the parties—represents a departure from ordinary arbitration practice which must be borne in mind by the parties' solicitors. The orders usually so made in this way relate to pleadings, further and better particulars, expert evidence, discovery, and date and place of hearing.

### Enforcement of orders

20–05    While in most respects there is no difference between the powers of an official referee arbitrator and any other arbitrator, it would appear that in one not unimportant respect official referees possess an authority denied to non-judicial arbitrators. By section 12 of the Arbitration

---

[4] See para. 7–10 above.
[5] In 1953 it was proposed that appeals from official referees sitting as arbitrators should go direct to the Court of Appeal, as in the case of other appeals from official referees. However this was rejected by the Evershed Committee and appeals continue to go to the Queen's Bench Division. See Committee on Supreme Court Practice and Procedure, Final report 1953, Cmd. 8878, para. 530.
[6] S.I. 1982 No. 1111.

Act 1950, and section 5(1) and (2) of the Arbitration Act 1979, the High Court has power to enforce the interlocutory orders of an arbitrator. Now Order 36, rule 4(1) provides by paragraph (*a*) that an official referee shall have the same jurisdiction powers and duties as a judge "for the purpose of disposing of any cause or matter (including any interlocutory application therein) or any other business referred to him."[7] No doubt an arbitration is not a cause or matter, but it would appear to be embraced by the words "any other business" and if this is so it would seem that the official referee himself has the power to enforce his interlocutory orders and that in his case it is unnecessary to make application in that regard to a Queen's Bench judge. Whether this result was is the mind of the draftsman of the relevant provisions may be doubted, and at the time of writing the question has not been tested by appeal. Professional opinion seems to be in favour of the interpretation here suggested.[8]

### A little used jurisdiction

Until recently this jurisdiction has not been widely used. Between 1935, when arbitration figures commenced to be given separately in the Judicial Statistics, and 1984 the highest number of cases brought in in any one year was three. Writing in 1970 the then senior official referee, Sir Walker Carter Q.C. said "This provision . . . has been surprisingly little used in recent years and the opportunity to obtain the services of an arbitrator and his clerk upon payment of a £6 fee has not often been taken."[9] The fee is now £30 for the entire hearing and when one contrasts this with the cost of securing a non-judicial arbitrator and providing him with a hall in which to sit, Sir Walker's surprise may be reiterated. It has been suggested that parties to arbitration agreements like to select an arbitrator of their choice, whereas the rota system prevents this. However the parties do know the identity of the permanent official referees, one of whom will be chosen; moreover the process is not dissimilar from the common device of having the arbitrator chosen by the President of a body such as the Law Society and such bodies have their own rotas. It has also been suggested[10] that parties are suspicious of the provisions of Order 36, rule 7(2) whereby a case may be transferred from one official referee to another. No doubt under this rule such a transfer could be effected without the parties' consent, but in practice such a transfer is highly unlikely: while the exigencies of the

**20–06**

---

[7] For the full wording see Appendix B below.

[8] *cf.* Russell, *The Law of Arbitration* (19th ed., 1979), p. 238. For a contrary view see Mustill & Boyd, *Commercial Arbitration* (1982), p. 237.

[9] *33 Atkin's Court Forms* (2nd ed.), p. 252.

[10] The jurisdiction is "little used, possibly due to the fact that a transfer might deprive the parties of the arbitrator whom they chose," Burrows, "Official Referees" (1940) 56 L.Q.R. 504 at 506.

moment sometimes require such mandatory transfer of litigation[11] the official referees regard the continuing identity of the referee-arbitrator as an important matter. However, although sparingly used, the procedure is far from obsolete, and it has been given new life by the decision of the Court of Appeal in *Crouch*.[12] As the Court there indicated, one way of surmounting an official referee's inability to apply the full powers of an arbitrator in construction contracts is to appoint him arbitrator under section 11.[13] That decision was in 1984: the number of section 11 arbitrations entered jumped to 11 in 1985 and 19 in 1986.[14]

### Provincial official referees as arbitrators

20–07    It is doubtful whether the provincial official referees, *i.e.* those assigned to circuits other than the south-eastern circuit, are able to act as arbitrators. This follows from the wording of paragraph (2) of Order 36, rule 5, providing that any application under section 11 of the Arbitration Act 1950, must be made to the referee to whom the reference has been allocated under paragraph (3) of that rule. Since paragraph (3) refers only to "official referees' business in the Royal Courts of Justice" it would follow that only the official referees operating in the Royal Courts of Justice, *i.e.* the London or south-eastern circuit official referees, may be required to arbitrate under section 11 of the Act of 1950.

### Construction arbitration appeals

20–08    One direct result of the *Crouch* decision is that, following the Master of the Rolls' suggestion that the official referees' court could adopt in relation to the construction industry the same role as that of the Commercial Court to commercial activities,[15] appeals from arbitrators in construction cases have been shifted from the Commercial Court to the official referees' court. This change has been effected administratively without any change in the rules. By R.S.C., Order 73, rules 2, 3 and 6, appeals from arbitrators' awards and applications for leave to bring such appeals must be heard by a Commercial judge "unless any such judge otherwise directs."[16] It is now the practice for all such applications for leave to appeal an award in a construction industry arbitration to be "otherwise directed" to the official referees' court. Applications still have to be made to the Commercial judge in the first instance. If the official referee gives leave the appeal is subsequently heard in the official referees' court. A curious and perhaps unforeseen

---

[11] See para. 13–02 above.
[12] [1984] Q.B. 644; see para. 6–08 above.
[13] *Ibid.* at 666.
[14] See Appendix F, Table 3, below, para. F–04.
[15] See para. 6–09 above.
[16] Ord. 73, r. 6.

result of this procedure is that where an official referee acts as arbitrator under section 11 of the Arbitration Act 1950, any application to appeal his award, and any appeal from his award, is heard by one of his brethren. It appears not unlikely that other applications to the Commercial Court in construction industry arbitrations (*e.g.* to set aside an award or remove an arbitrator) would be similarly directed to be heard by official referees.

## Proposed amendment to the jurisdiction

Both the Official Referees' Users' Committee and the Departmental    **20–09** Committee on Arbitration ("the Mustill Committee") have recommended that section 11 of the Arbitration Act 1950, be repealed and replaced by a provision enabling official referees to sit as judicial arbitrators on the same basis as High Court judges.[17]

---

[17] First Report of the Official Referees' Users' Committee, para. 5–2.

# Part IV
# The Future

# Chapter 21
# Progress

## A time of change

The 1980s have been a significant time of progress for the official **21–01** referees' courts. A momentous change was the introduction in 1982 of direct access for litigants to the court by marking their writs "official referees' business." No longer had they to apply for the exercise of another court's discretion when they wished to utilise the expertise of the official referees. No longer were the judges solely "referees," and thus was broken down the principal distinction between official referees and other judges trying High Court civil cases.

Equal in importance was the setting up of the Official Referees' Users' Committee. This has proved to be an energetic and influential body. Its formation is not unconnected with the two other salient improvements in the 1980s in the courts: the doubling of its establishment from three to six judges in 1983–1984 and the provision of a suitable home for the courts, their officials and their clients due to take place in 1988. The former has removed the reproach that the delays in the official referees courts were "wholly unacceptable"[1] and it is to be hoped that the latter will remove the astonishment with which litigants reacted to the cramped conditions in which the majority of the courts sat.

Other changes have been advocated by the Users' Committee, relating to archaic or obsolete provisions in the rules. Another change which might well be considered would be the promotion of greater liaison or integration with the provincial official referees, who now bear an increasing share of the workload.[2] The changes, actual or prospective, are seen to emphasise the important place of the official referees' court in the despatch of High Court business.

---

[1] *Per* Donaldson M.R. in the *Crouch* case, para. 6–08 above.
[2] Provincial official referees deal with nearly one-third of the country's official referee cases: see para. 15–04 above, n.10.

### "An important part . . . "

**21–02**    When in the House of Commons on March 30, 1984 the Attorney General, Sir Michael Havers, referred to the official referees' courts as "an important part of the administration of justice, although clearly one about which not much is known"[3] he touched on two different but crucial matters. Importance can hardly be denied to a court which deploys six to ten judges or deputy judges at a time and which entertains over 1,000 cases and hears over 4,000 summonses annually. Judged by the quantity of work done it is in the forefront of the specialist courts within the High Court. This important status has come about because from its earliest days the court has attracted work from what is now considered to be the largest industry in the country, the construction industry.

### The construction industry court

**21–03**    The construction industry generates a good deal of litigation, both in the High Court and before arbitrators. To serve this process there exist numerous firms of specialist solicitors and a strong and growing specialist bar. That a specialist court is called for in this class of litigation is evident when one considers both the intricate and detailed nature of the evidence in such disputes and the complicated wording in which the industry clothes its contracts. Construction and allied work has always provided the majority of the cases in the official referees' lists but of recent years the proportion has risen and is now thought to be about 85 per cent. Hence the court has for many years been accepted as the specialist court of the construction industry, a fact now emphasised by the transfer to them of construction arbitration appeals[4] and the institution of a series of law reports devoted to recording official referees' decisions in construction cases.[5] While it must not be forgotten that the court has a minority of cases unconnected with construction and its ancillaries of dilapidations and building professional negligence cases, it is as the construction industry court that its future clearly lies. The decision in *Crouch*[6] represented a setback in this process, diverting some work to arbitration, but the inevitable loss of some cases has been offset by an expansion in the work generally; the total intake has continued to increase since that decision.[7]

---

[3] On the occasion referred to in para. 4–08 above; *Hansard* (6th series), vol. 57, col. 626.
[4] See para. 20–08 above.
[5] See para. 13–10 above.
[6] See para. 6–08 above.
[7] See Table 1 in Appendix F, below, para. F–01.

## "About which not much is known"

No Attorney-General ever used more apt words than Sir Michael   **21–04**
Havers when he applied the above phrase to the official referees' courts
as mentioned in paragraph 21–02, above. The official referees have long
suffered from a lack of knowledge and understanding of the nature,
size, and importance of their work. Many lawyers share these attri-
butes, as witness the slow response to the opening up of the court to
direct access by writ.[8] Official circles appear to have shared this ignorance. The Beeching commission's attitude to the official referees was
much resented at the time, and one of the top salaries review bodies
recommended the abolition of the official referees' salary lead over
other circuit judges on the ground that any circuit judge could do the
work. The general misapprehension may stem from some legal folk
memory of the early unhallowed days recorded in Chapter 3 above.
Whatever the cause there remains an unspoken feeling that this court is
to be differentiated from other parts of the High Court, and differentiated to its disadvantage. If one looks for a reason for this attitude it
must be found in the past.

## A legacy of the past

If one looks back over the history of this court from its inception in   **21–05**
1873 to today one sees that in a peculiarly haphazard and English way
the tribunal which was instituted to provide a mode of trial alternative
to jury trial has transformed itself into one of the specialist courts of the
High Court of Justice. Had it not done so it would have died long ago;
there is no need for referees to stand in the place of juries as finders of
fact now that the judges have taken over fact-finding and the civil jury
has virtually disappeared. But there is one legacy from the court's past
which still hinders it. Because it started as a subordinate tribunal its
judges are still subordinate in rank and in pay. Alone of permanent
judges in the High Court they are not High Court judges. This is said to
cause recruitment difficulties, and whether or not that is so, one effect is
to interpose a financial barrier between the specialist construction bar
and the official referees' bench. A practitioner at the specialist patent
bar, or Admiralty bar, or commercial bar may be attracted to become a
judge of the court wherein he is skilled; the attraction for members of
the construction bar is far less, or some might say non-existent in view
of the fact that the leaders in this field are among the top earners at the
bar today.

---

[8] After five years less than one-third of cases were so started: Appendix F, Table 1A,
below, para. F–02.

### The future

**21–06**     But the element of subordination or inferiority may be on the way out. Some of the special characteristics distinguishing the court from other courts[9] are disappearing. The need for reference has gone. The immunity from appeal on fact is under attack: the Users' Committee has recommended that there should be a general right of appeal, with leave.[10] A remaining central characteristic is the assignment from the outset of a case to a named judge who follows it through directions to trial. This concept stems historically from the practice of arbitrators and for some years the official referees have been moving away from it. Although lip service may be paid to the value of one judge taking a case under his wing from inception to judgment,[11] in practice the procedure is not necessarily adhered to. A litigant may find his summons being taken by another judge if his judge is out of town or indisposed, and he may find a recorder, a deputy, or another official referee trying his case owing to the exigencies of listing. No one seems any the worse for this. It is to be noted that the Court of Appeal's decision in *Crouch*[12] furthers this process of assimilation. That case not only decided that the High Court could not use certain special powers conferred by a contract upon an arbitrator, but also that the powers of an official referee were those of a High Court judge, no more and—by inference—no less. It is the writer's view that the practice of the official referees to operate those special powers was a tradition handed down from the early days when the official referees thought of themselves as arbitrators. That tradition has been given its quietus by *Crouch*, a decision in line in this respect with the forthright observations of Brandon L.J. mentioned at paragraph 11–02.[13] It would be in line with this view if the assignment to a named judge, at present enshrined in Order 36, were to be abolished. That may lie far in the future, but meanwhile it can be seen that uniformity of procedure is being promoted either, as in the above instances, by discouraging quirks of procedure, or by applying to other courts innovations pioneered by the official referees, such as the exchange of experts reports, the compulsory meeting of experts, and the exchange of witnesses' statements. Either way, differences between the official referees' courts and the other courts are being dismantled.

No doubt all such matters will have been considered in the current

---

[9] See the characteristics listed at para. 1–06 above.
[10] First Report of Official Referees' Users' Committee, para. 4.2.
[11] *e.g. per* Forbes J. in *Durston* v. *O'Keefe* [1974] 1 W.L.R. 777 at 779, cited at para. 7–06 above.
[12] Summarised at para. 6–08 above.
[13] And see *Renown Investment Holdings Ltd.* v. *F. Shepherd & Son Ltd.* (1976) 120 S.J. 840, where building cases were held not to be distinguishable from other heavy Queen's Bench cases.

Civil Justice Review. If the court remains in its present form it is to be hoped that it will be given a new name. To call its judges "official referees" was thought to be "not very satisfactory" as long ago as the Evershed Report (1953).[14] The present writer is proud to have been, and to have been called, an official referee, but he has in the end come to the conclusion that while the title remains, albeit unofficially, a whiff of the old status of inferiority will remain and that its abolition should be part of the process of bringing the official referees' court and judges into parity with the other parts of the High Court.

[14] See quotation at para. 4–05 above.

# Appendices

# Appendix A
# Statutes

## ARBITRATION ACT 1950

### (14 Geo. 6, c. 27)

**Reference to official referee**

**11.** Where an arbitration agreement provides that the reference shall **A–01** be to an official referee, any official referee to whom application is made shall, subject to any order of the High Court or a judge thereof as to transfer or otherwise, hear and determine the matters agreed to be referred.

## SUPREME COURT ACT 1981

### (c. 54)

[Printed as amended by s.59(1) of the Administration of Justice Act 1982, c. 53]

**Exercise of High Court jurisdiction otherwise than by judges of that court**

**68.** (1) Provision may be made by rules of court as to the cases in **A–02** which jurisdiction of the High Court may be exercised by—

 (*a*) such Circuit judges, deputy Circuit judges or Recorders as the Lord Chancellor may from time to time nominate to deal with official referees' business;
 (*b*) special referees; or
 (*c*) masters, registrars, district registrars or other officers of the court.

(2) Without prejudice to the generality of subsection (1) rules of court may in particular—

 (*a*) authorise the whole of any cause or matter, or any question or issue therein, to be tried before any such person as is mentioned in that subsection; or

(b) authorise any question arising in any cause or matter to be referred to any such person for inquiry and report.

(3) Rules of court shall not authorise the exercise of powers of attachment and committal to any such person as is mentioned in subsection (1)(b) or (c).

(4) Subject to subsection (5) the decision of any such person as is mentioned in subsection (1) may be called in question in such manner as may be prescribed by rules of court, whether by appeal to the Court of Appeal, or by appeal or application to a divisional court or a judge in court or a judge in chambers, or by an adjournment to a judge in court or a judge in chambers.

(5) Rules of court may provide either generally or to a limited extent for decisions of persons nominated under subsection (1)(a) being called in question only by appeal on a question of law.

(6) The cases in which jurisdiction of the High Court may be exercised by persons nominated under subsection (1)(a) shall be known as "official referees' business"; and, subject to rules of court, the distribution of official referees' business among persons so nominated shall be determined in accordance with directions given by the Lord Chancellor.

(7) Any reference to an official referee in any enactment, whenever passed, or in rules of court or any other instrument or document, whenever made, shall, unless the context otherwise requires, be construed as, or (where the context requires) as including, a reference to a person nominated under subsection (1)(a).

# Appendix B
# Rules of the Supreme Court

## ORDER 1

### Citation, Application, Interpretation and Forms

### Definitions

**4.**—(1) In these rules, unless the context otherwise requires, the fol-  **B–01**
lowing expressions have the meanings hereby respectively assigned to
them, namely:

> . . . "official referee" means a person nominated under section
> 68(1)(*a*) of the Act; . . .

## ORDER 25

### Summons for Directions

### Summons for directions

**1.**—(2) This rule applies to all actions begun by writ except—  **B–02**

> (*g*) actions which have been commenced, or ordered to be tried as,
> official referees' business. . . .

## ORDER 33

### Place and Mode of Trial

### Mode of trial

**2.** Subject to the provisions of these rules, a cause or matter, or any  **B–03**
question or issue arising therein, may be tried before:

> (*d*) an official referee with or without the assistance of assessors,
> or . . .

## ORDER 36

### TRIALS BEFORE, AND INQUIRIES BY, REFEREES AND MASTERS

### Application and interpretation

B–04    **1.**—(1) This Order applies to official referees' business in the Chancery Division or Queen's Bench Division, and the other provisions of these rules apply to such business subject to the provisions of this Order.

(2) In this Order official referees' business includes, without prejudice to any right to a trial with a jury, any cause or matter commenced in the Chancery Division or Queen's Bench Division, being a cause or matter:

(*a*) which involves a prolonged examination of documents or accounts, or a technical scientific or local investigation such as could more conveniently be conducted by an official referee; or

(*b*) for which trial by an official referee is desirable in the interests of one or more of the parties on grounds of expedition, economy or convenience or otherwise.

### Commencement of official referees' business

B–05    **2.**—(1) Before the issue of a writ or originating summons by which official referees' business is to be begun, it may be marked in the top left hand corner with the words "official referees' business" and, on the issue of the writ or summons so marked, the cause or matter begun thereby shall be treated as official referees' business.

(2) If the plaintiff intends to issue a writ or originating summons for service out of the jurisdiction and to mark it in accordance with paragraph (1), an application for leave to issue the writ or summons and to serve it out of the jurisdiction may be made to an official referee.

(3) The affidavit in support of an application under paragraph (2) must, in addition to the matters required to be stated by Order 11, rule 4(1), state that the plaintiff intends to mark the writ or summons in accordance with paragraph (1) of this rule.

(4) If the official referee hearing an application under paragraph (2) is of opinion that the cause or matter should not be dealt with as official referees' business, he may adjourn the application to be heard by a master.

### Transfer of official referees' business

B–06    **3.**—(1) At any stage before the trial of a cause or matter in the Chancery Division or Queen's Bench Division, any party may apply by summons to the Court to transfer the proceedings to be dealt with as official referees' business.

146

(2) If the Court considers that any cause or matter in the Chancery Division or Queen's Bench Division may more appropriately be dealt with as official referees' business, the Court may of its own motion, but subject to any right to a trial with a jury, order that the cause or matter, or any question or issue of fact arising therein, shall be tried by an official referee.

(3) An official referee may of his own motion or on the application of any party, order a cause or matter which is proceeding as official referees' business to be transferred to the Chancery Division or Queen's Bench Division if he considers that it may more appropriately be tried by a master or judge.

(4) No order for the transfer of proceedings shall be made by the Court or an official referee under this rule unless the parties have either:

> (*a*) had an opportunity of being heard on the issue, or
> (*b*) consented to such an order.

### Powers, etc. of official referees

**4.**—(1) Subject to any directions contained in the order referring any business to an official referee—    **B–07**

> (*a*) the official referee shall for the purpose of disposing of any cause or matter (including any interlocutory application therein) or any other business referred to him have the same jurisdiction, powers and duties (including the power of committal and discretion as to costs) as a judge, exercisable or, as the case may be, to be performed as nearly as circumstances admit in the like cases, in the like manner and subject to the like limitations; and
> (*b*) every trial and all other proceedings before an official referee shall, as nearly as circumstances admit, be conducted in the like manner as the like proceedings before a judge.

(2) Without prejudice to the generality of paragraph (1), but subject to any such directions as are mentioned therein, an official referee before whom any cause or matter is tried shall have the like powers as the Court with respect to claims relating to or connected with the original subject-matter of the cause or matter by any party thereto against any other person, and Order 15, rule 5 (2) and Order 16 shall with any necessary modifications apply in relation to any such claim accordingly.

(3) An official referee may hold any trial or any other proceeding before him at any place which appears to him to be convenient and may adjourn the proceedings from place to place as he thinks fit.

### Allocation of business to official referees

B–08     **5.**—(1) No writ or originating summons by which official referees' business is to be begun and no order referring any business to an official referee under these rules shall specify any particular referee.

(2) Any application under section 11 of the Arbitration Act 1950, to an official referee shall be made to the referee to whom the reference has been allocated under paragraph (3) or any other official referee to whom the reference has been transferred under the following provisions of this Order.

(3) Official referees' business in the Royal Courts of Justice shall be allocated by the rota clerk to official referees in rotation.

### Entry of business and application for directions

B–09     **6.**—(1) An application for directions (including an application for a fixed date of hearing) shall be made by the plaintiff to the official referee to whom the business has been allocated within 14 days of—

>     (*a*)  the giving by a defendant of notice of intention to defend, or
>     (*b*)  the date of the order transferring the cause or matter,

whichever is the later.

(2) If that party does not make an application for directions to the official referee in accordance with paragraph (1), any other interested party may do so or may apply to the official referee—

>     (*a*)  in the case of any cause or matter referred for trial, for an order to strike out the pleadings of the party in default or, where the party in default is the plaintiff or has made a counterclaim, an order to dismiss the action or counterclaim;
>     (*b*)  in the case of any question or issue referred for trial or inquiry and report, to have the matter referred back to the Court.

(3) Upon application by any party for an order under paragraph (2) (*a*), the official referee may make the order asked for on such terms as may be just or deal with the application as if it were an application for directions.

(4) Order 25, rules 2 to 7, shall, with the omission of so much of rule 7 (1) as requires parties to serve a notice specifying the orders and directions which they desire and with any other necessary modifications, apply as if any application under this rule were a summons for directions under that Order.

### Transfer of business from one official referee to another

B–10     **7.**—(1) If, in the opinion of the Lord Chancellor or the Lord Chief Justice, it is expedient so to do having regard to the state of the business pending before the official referees, he may order the transfer of any

148

business from any official referee to any other official referee.

(2) Any official referee may order the transfer of any business from himself to any other official referee who consents to the transfer.

(3) In the absence, or with the consent, of the official referee to whom any business was allocated or has been transferred, any interlocutory application may be made to any other official referee and that other referee may deal with the application and make any order thereon which could have been made by the first-mentioned referee.

### Reference to official referee of question of fact for inquiry, etc.

**8.** In any cause or matter in the Chancery Division or Queen's Bench Division other than a criminal proceeding by the Crown the Court may, subject to any right to a trial with a jury, refer to an official referee for inquiry and report any question or issue of fact arising therin; and, unless the Court otherwise orders, the further consideration of the cause or matter shall stand adjourned until the receipt of the official referee's report. **B–11**

### Report on reference under rule 8

**9.**—(1) The report made by an official referee in pursuance of a reference under rule 8 shall be made to the Court and notice thereof served on the parties to the reference. **B–12**

(2) The official referee may in his report submit any question arising therein for the decision of the Court or make a special statement of facts from which the Court may draw such inferences as it thinks fit.

(3) On the receipt of the official referee's report, the Court may—

 (a) adopt the report in whole or in part;

 (b) vary the report;

 (c) require an explanation from him;

 (d) remit the whole or any part of the question or issue originally referred to him for further consideration by him or any other official referee; or

 (e) decide the question or issue originally referred to him on the evidence taken before him, either with or without additional evidence.

(4) When the report of the official referee has been made, an application to vary the report or remit the whole or any part of the question or issue originally referred may be made on the hearing by the Court of the further consideration of the cause or matter, after giving not less than 4 days' notice thereof, and any other application with respect to the report may be made on that hearing without notice.

(5) Where on a reference under rule 8 the Court orders that the further

149

consideration of the cause or matter in question shall not stand adjourned until the receipt of the official referee's report, the order may contain directions with respect to the proceedings on the receipt of the report, and the foregoing provisions of this rule shall have effect subject to any such directions.

**10. [Trial before, and enquiry by special referee].** . . .

**11. [Trial before, and inquiry by, master].** . . .

### Restriction of power to order trial before referee, etc.

B–13    **12.** Notwithstanding anything in this Order, no cause or matter to which Her Majesty or the Duke of Cornwall is a party or any question or issue therein shall be tried before an official referee except with the consent of Her Majesty or the Duke of Cornwall, as the case may be, and no question or issue in such cause or matter shall be referred for inquiry and report to a referee or master except with such consent.

### ORDER 37

### Damages: Assessment after Judgment and Orders for Provisional Damages

### Power to order assessment by referee, etc.

B–14    **4.**—(1) Where judgment is given in the Chancery Division or the Queen's Bench Division for damages to be assessed, the Court may—

(*a*) order that the assessment of the damages be referred to an official referee or to a special referee, or. . . .

### Assessment of value

B–15    **5.** The foregoing provisions of this Order shall apply in relation to a judgment for the value of goods to be assessed, with or without damages to be assessed, as they apply to a judgment for damages to be assessed, and references in those provisions to the assessment of damages shall be construed accordingly.

### Assessment of damages to time of assessment

B–16    **6.** Where damages are to be assessed (whether under this Order or otherwise) in respect of any continuing cause of action, they shall be assessed down to the time of the assessment.

150

## ORDER 38

### EVIDENCE

### Exchange of witnesses' statements

**2A.**—(1) This rule applies to any cause or matter which is proceeding **B–17** in the Chancery Division, the Commercial Court, the Admiralty Court or as official referees' business and in this rule "the Court" includes an official referee.

(2) At any stage in any cause or matter to which this rule applies the Court may, if it thinks fit for the purpose of disposing fairly and expeditiously of the cause or matter and saving costs, direct any party to serve on the other parties, on such terms as the Court shall think just, written statements of the oral evidence which the party intends to lead on any issues of fact to be decided at the trial.

(3) Directions given under paragraph (2) may—

(*a*) make different provision with regard to different issues of fact or different witnesses;

(*b*) require any written statement served to be signed by the intended witness;

(*c*) require that statements be filed with the Court.

(4) Subject to paragraph (6), where the party serving a statement under paragraph (2) does not call the witness to whose evidence it relates no other party may put the statement in evidence at the trial.

(5) Subject to paragraph (6) and unless the Court otherwise orders where the party serving the statement does call such a witness at the trial—

(*a*) the party may not without the consent of the other parties or the leave of the Court lead evidence from that witness the substance of which is not included in the statement served, except in relation to new matters which have arisen in the course of the trial;

(*b*) the Court may, on such terms as it thinks fit, direct that the statement served, or part of it, shall stand as the evidence in chief of the witness or part of such evidence;

(*c*) whether or not the statement or any part of it is referred to during the evidence in chief of the witness, any party may put the statement or any part of it in cross-examination of that witness.

(6) Where any statement served is one to which the Civil Evidence Acts 1968 and 1972 apply, paragraphs (4) and (5) shall take effect subject to the provisions of those Acts and Parts III and IV of this Order. The service of a statement pursuant to a direction given under paragraph (2)

shall not, unless expressly so stated by the party serving the same, be treated as a notice under the said Acts.

(7) Where a party fails to comply with a direction given under paragraph (2) he shall not be entitled to adduce evidence to which such direction related without the leave of the Court.

(8) Nothing in this rule shall deprive any party of his right to treat any communication as privileged or make admissible evidence otherwise inadmissible.

ORDER 58

Appeals from Masters, Registrars, Referees and Judges

### Appeals from official referees

B–18    **4.**—(1) Subject to paragraph (2) an appeal shall lie to the Court of Appeal—

> (*a*) from a decision of an official referee on a point of law or as to costs only; and
>
> (*b*) from a decision of an official referee on a question of fact relevant to a charge of fraud or breach of professional duty.

(2) In relation to any decision of an official referee referred to in paragraph (1), section 18 of the Act shall apply as if the official referee were a judge of the High Court.

(3) Except as provided by paragraph (1), and section 13 of the Administration of Justice Act 1960 (which provides for an appeal in cases of contempt of court), no judgment order or decision of an official referee in relation to any cause, matter, question or issue ordered to be tried before him shall be called in question by appeal or otherwise.

ORDER 59

Appeals to the Court of Appeal

### Application of Order to appeals

B–19    **1.** This Order applies, subject to the provisions of these rules with respect to particular appeals, to every appeal to the Court of Appeal (including so far as it is applicable thereto, any appeal to that Court from an official referee, master or other officer of the Supreme Court or from any tribunal from which an appeal lies to that Court under or by virtue of any enactment) not being an appeal for which other provision is made by these rules, and references to "the Court below" apply to any court, tribunal or person from which such an appeal lies.

## Documents to be lodged by appellant

**9.** (1) Not more than 14 days after the appeal first appears in a list to **B–20** be called "the List of Forthcoming Appeals" the appellant must cause to be lodged with the registrar the number of copies for which paragraph (2) provides of each of the following documents, namely—

    (*a*)  the notice of appeal;

    (*b*)  the respondent's notice;

    (*c*)  any supplementary notice served under rule 7;

    (*d*)  the judgment or order of the court below;

    (*e*)  the originating process by which the proceedings in the court below were begun, any interlocutory or other related process which is the subject of the appeal, the pleadings (including particulars) if any, and, in the case of an appeal in an Admiralty cause or matter, the preliminary acts, if any;

    (*f*)  the transcript of the official shorthand note or record, if any, of the judge's reasons for giving the judgment or making the order of the court below, or in the absence of such a note or record, the judge's note of his reasons or, if the judge's note is not available, counsel's note of the judge's reasons approved wherever possible by the judge;

    (*g*)  such part of the transcript of the official shorthand note or record, if any, of the evidence given in the court below as are relevant to any question at issue on the appeal or, in the absence of such a note or record, such parts of the judge's note of the evidence as are relevant to any such question;

    (*h*)  any list of exhibits made under Order 35, rule 11, or the schedule of evidence, as the case may be;

    (*i*)  such affidavits, exhibits, or parts of exhibits, as were in evidence in the court below and as are relevant to any question at issue on the appeal.

(2) Unless otherwise directed the number of copies to be lodged in accordance with paragraph (1) is three copies except—

    (*a*)  where the appeal is to be heard by two judges in which case it is two copies; or . . .

    (*b*)  in the case of an appeal in an Admiralty cause or matter in which case it is four copies or, if the Court of Appeal is to hear the appeal with assessors, six.

(2A) When the transcripts, if any, referred to in items (*f*) and (*g*) of paragraph (1) have been bespoken by the appellant and paid for, the number of such transcripts required in accordance with paragraph (2) shall be sent by the official shorthand writer or transcriber direct to the registrar.

(3) At any time after an appeal has been set down in accordance with rule 5 the registrar may give such directions in relation to the documents to be prodced at the appeal, and the manner in which they are to be presented, and as to other matters incidental to the conduct of the appeal, as appear best adapted to secure the just, expeditious and economical disposal of the appeal.

(4) The directions referred to in paragraph (3) may be given without a hearing provided always that the registrar may at any time issue a summons requiring the parties to an appeal to attend before him and any party to an appeal may apply at any time for an appointment before the registrar.

### General powers of the Court

B–21    10.—(1) In relation to an appeal the Court of Appeal shall have all the powers and duties as to amendment and otherwise of the High Court including, without prejudice to the generality of the foregoing words, the powers of the Court under Order 36 to refer any question or issue of fact for trial before, or inquiry and report by, an official referee.

In relation to a reference made to an official referee, any thing required or authorised under Order 36, rule 9, to be done by, or before the Court shall be done by, to or before the Court of Appeal.

(2) . . .

ORDER 64

SITTINGS, VACATIONS AND OFFICE HOURS

### Sittings of the Supreme Court

B–22    1.—(1) The sittings of the Court of Appeal and of the High Court shall be four in every year, that is to say—

(a) the Michaelmas sittings which shall begin on 1st October and end on 21st December;

(b) the Hilary sittings which shall begin on 11th January and end on the Wednesday before Easter Sunday;

(c) the Easter sittings which shall begin on the second Tuesday after Easter Sunday and end on the Friday before the spring holiday; and

(d) the Trinity sittings which shall begin on the second Tuesday after the spring holiday and end on 31st July.

(2) In this rule "spring holiday" means the bank holiday falling on the last Monday in May or any day appointed instead of that day under section 1(2) of the Banking and Financial Dealings Act 1971.

## Sittings of official referees: applications in Long Vacation

**6.**—(1) The sittings of the official referees shall be those specified in rule 1, but nothing in this rule shall prevent an official referee from sitting in vacation if he thinks it expedient so to do.

(2) Any interlocutory orders or directions required in connection with a cause or matter pending before an official referee may in the Long Vacation be made or given by a master of the Queen's Bench Division.

## ORDER 68

### OFFICIAL SHORTHAND NOTE

## Trial before official referee

**7.**—(1) If in a reference for a trial before an official referee the referee **B–23** certifies that it is desirable for an official shorthand note to be taken, such a note shall be taken of the evidence given orally in court and of any judgment delivered by the referee.

(2) Where such a note has been taken, the provisions of this Order relating to transcripts shall apply in relation to the reference as they apply in relation to proceedings before a judge.

# Appendix C
# Practice Directions

A. **The Senior Official Referee's Practice Direction of July 8, 1968** [1968] 1 W.L.R. 1425; [1968] 2 All E.R. 1213.

## OFFICIAL REFEREES

C–01    1. At the time of the issue of the first summons before the Official Referee, a copy of all the pleadings, including particulars, already served should be lodged with his clerk so that they can be considered by the Official Referee before the hearing of the summons. Such copy of the pleadings may be collected from the clerk to the Official Referee for the purpose of preparing a bound copy of the pleadings for use at the trial.

2. At the hearing of the first summons before the Official Referee, the solicitors of the parties or their London Agents should be in the position to state the nature of the claim and of the defence. Failure in this respect may result in unnecessary adjournments with attendant costs.

3. At the hearing of the first summons before him, the Official Referee will give the necessary directions and made the necessary orders regarding the steps in the action to be taken by the parties. It is of the utmost importance that these steps should be taken within the time-limits set by the diection or order, so that the practice of giving a fixed date for the trial may be continued.

4. Once an action has been given a fixed date for trial, no alteration will be granted except with the leave of the Official Referee which will be granted only in exceptional circumstances. If a fixed date for trial is vacated, the fresh date for trial may not be a fixed date.

5. Where a party intends to adduce expert evidence, he should produce to the other party his expert's statement of proposed evidence, together with any reports, plans, models, calculations, etc., relevant to it, for agreement if possible. Failing such agreement, the other party should deliver to the first party a written statement setting out particulars of the matters not agreed. When both parties intend to adduce

expert evidence, each should follow this procedure. Failure by any party to follow this procedure may result in a special order as to costs.

WALKER CARTER,
Senior Official Referee.

July 8, 1968.

NOTE: Direction No. 5 has been overtaken by the Rules of the Supreme Court and is now obsolete. See para 8–10, above n 1.

## B. **The Current Procedure Notice.**

### HIGH COURT OF JUSTICE

### OFFICIAL REFEREES' BUSINESS

### PROCEDURE (ORDER 36 R.S.C.)

**1.** Bring to Room 747 (Rota Clerk) the following:—

C–02

(a) Original Writ or Originating Summons and a copy

(b) Original Order (if any) referring the matter and a copy

(c) Praecipe E.26 (from Room 278), stamped £30 (unless the action has been previously set down for trial elsewhere and the fee was paid then. In this case, the document carrying the fee should be lodged with the Rota Clerk) (The matter will then be allocated to a particular Official Referee)

(d) 2 copies of a Judge's Summons (Form S.1), 1 stamped £15. (Suitable wording being; " . . . for further [or General] directions . . .")

(e) Copy pleadings (one set starting with a further copy of the Writ or Originating Summons).

**2.** All summonses will be issued by the Rota Clerk, stamped with the fee of £15 each and should be lodged in duplicate. The following endorsement shall be completed before a date may be given:—

I/we estimate summons will not exceed . . . hrs. . . . mins. with/without counsel. Any change to be notified to rota clerk immediately.

**3.** All orders to be drawn up should be brought (in duplicate) with the summons carrying the endorsement, to the clerk to the Official Referee to whom the matter has been allocated.

NOTE: By the time of publication this Notice will have been rendered inaccurate by reason of the court's removal to St. Dunstan's House. A revised Notice will be issued, obtainable at the official referees' office at St. Dunstan's House, Fetter Lane, London EC4.

## C. The Northern Circuit Practice Direction of October 9, 1985

### NORTHERN CIRCUIT

### ARRANGEMENTS FOR THE CONDUCT OF OFFICIAL REFEREES' BUSINESS

C–03   1. [Names of nominated judges]

2. In the interest of uniformity, the conduct of such business shall continue to be co-ordinated within the District Registries of Liverpool and Manchester. A member of the staff of each of these District Registries has been assigned to act in such matters as Clerk to the Circuit Judge dealing with official referees' business.

3. If a District Registrar orders that a cause or matter shall be dealt with as official referees' business, or a writ is issued marked "official referees' business," the District Registrar will direct at which District Registry, Liverpool or Manchester, the reference will be conducted. The papers will thereupon be sent, without any further directions, to the appropriate Registry.

4. Subject to any different specific direction by a Courts Administrator, cases which are referred to the Liverpool District Registry will be assigned to His Honour Judge J. A. Stannard and those referred to the Manchester District Registry will be assigned to His Honour Judge D. G. F. Franks. This will be without prejudice to the power of each of these Judges to order the transfer of any case to the other of them, or to one of the Judges taking official referees' business in London, if that Judge consents.

5. In the ordinary course the giving of directions, the hearing of other interlocutory applications and trial will take place in Liverpool in cases which are referred to the Liverpool District Registry and in Manchester in cases which are referred to the Manchester District Registry. However Their Honours Judges Franks and Stannard have stated that if the parties consent to such a course and can agree upon the orders which are to be made they are prepared to consider dealing with directions and other interlocutory applications by correspondence, and in appropriate cases, and so far as possible, directions will be given for trial wherever is most convenient within the boundaries of the Circuit, taking into account the convenience of the parties and witnesses.

# Appendix D
# Scott Schedules

## Scott Schedule in a Dilapidations Case

IN THE HIGH COURT OF JUSTICE
QUEEN'S BENCH DIVISION
BEFORE HIS HONOUR JUDGE Z, OFFICIAL REFEREE

1983 A. No. 1000

Between:       A. B.              Plaintiff

               and

               X. Y.              Defendant

### PLAINTIFF'S SCOTT SCHEDULE

Delivered pursuant to the Order of His Honour Judge 2 dated the 1st
March 1983

| 1<br>Item<br>no. | 2<br>Plaintiff's descrip-<br>tion of each<br>item of disrepair | 3<br>Plaintiff's<br>costs | 4<br>Defendant's<br>comments | 5<br>Defendant's<br>costs | 6<br>For<br>official<br>referee |
|---|---|---|---|---|---|
| 1 | All exterior woodwork to be repainted. | £2,000 | Admitted | £1,500 | |
| 2 | All exterior brickwork to be repointed. | £2,500 | Denied: unnecessary | £1,500 | |
| 3 | 50 slates approx. damaged or displaced; to be replaced or renewed. | £300 | Not more than 10 slates need attention | 10 slates: £50<br>50 slates: £150 | |
| 4 | Make up worn access path to front door. | £50 | Denied: not within covenant to repair. | £10 | |
| 5 | etc. | | | | |

Delivered by the Plaintiff the 1st day of April 1983.
Delivered by the Defendant the 1st day of May 1983.

D–02

FORM 2

Scott Schedule in claim by Building Owner against Main Contractor (First Defendant),
Sub-Contractor (Second Defendant) and Architect (Third Defendant)

| 1 Item no. | 2 Para. no. in Specification | 3 Plaintiff's case | 4 Against which Def't | 5 Plaintiff's damages | 6 First Defendant's comments | 7 Second Defendant's comments | 8 Third Defendant's comments | 9 For O.R. |
|---|---|---|---|---|---|---|---|---|
| 1 | 100 | Roof glazing to Bay 3 improperly sealed; roof leaks. | 1st and 2nd | £5,000 | Work done by Second Defendant, whose comments are adopted | Work was left watertight | N/A | |
| 2 | 105 | Door from office 5 to offices 6 and 7 foul each other when opened; design defect. | 3rd | £100 | N/A | N/A | Denied: door from office 5 to office 6 was hung wrong way round | |
| 3 | 110 | $\frac{1}{2}$" subsidence in west wall of garage due to insufficient foundations | 1st and 3rd | £1,250 | Foundations as per drawings; design defect. | N/A | 18" footings as designed were sufficient; inferior concrete mix used by 1st Defendant | |
| 4 | etc. | | | | | | | |

NOTE. Heading and subscription as in Form 1.

## FORM 3

### Plaintiff's Scott Schedule for Goods Sold and Delivered

**D–03**

| 1<br>Item<br>no. | 2<br>Invoice<br>no. | 3<br>Delivery<br>date | 4<br>Description<br>of goods | 5<br>Price | 6<br>Defendant's<br>comments | 7<br>For official<br>referee |
|---|---|---|---|---|---|---|
| 1 | 100 | 1/1/83 | 10 gross electric batteries | £380 | No such consignment received | |
| 2 | 102 | 1/2/83 | 12 doz. electric torches, type XYZ | £200 | Received damaged and rejected. Returned on 5/2/83 | |
| 3 | 104 | 1/3/83 | 100 bicycle rear lamps | £140 | 2 lamps defective and unsaleable: deduct £2 | |
| 4 | etc. | | | | | |

NOTE. Heading and subscription as in Form 1.

## FORM 4

### Builder's Scott Schedule for Extras

**D–04**

| 1<br>Item<br>no. | 2<br>Description<br>of work | 3<br>Amount<br>claimed | 4<br>Defendant's<br>comments | 5<br>Defendant's<br>price | 6<br>For official<br>referee |
|---|---|---|---|---|---|
| 1 | Making good plaster to walls of best bedroom | £200 | Price excessive | £100 | |
| 2 | Extra cost of gloss paint to woodwork of drawing room | £150 | Denied: included in fixed price contract—see Specification, item 10 | £150 | |
| 3 | etc. | | | | |

NOTE. Heading and subscription as in Form 1.

# Appendix E
# The Official Referees

**E–01**   James ANDERSON Q.C. 1876–1886
George DOWDESWELL Q.C. 1876–1889
Charles ROUPELL 1876–1889
Sir Henry VEREY 1876–1920
Rt. Hon. Sir Edward RIDLEY 1886–1897
G. W. HEMMING Q.C. 1889–1905
Sir Edward POLLOCK 1897–1927
Montague MUIR-MACKENZIE 1905–1919
Sir Francis NEWBOLT K.C. 1920–1936
George Alexander SCOTT 1920–1933
Sir William HANSELL K.C. 1927–1931
Sir Ronald BOSANQUET K.C. 1931–1954
Charles PITMAN K.C. 1933–1945
Sir Tom EASTHAM K.C. 1936–1954
John TRAPNELL K.C. 1943–1949
Herbert SAMUELS K.C. 1945–1947
Sir Brett CLOUTMAN V.C., Q.C. 1948–1963
Sir Lionel LEACH Q.C. 1948–1956
Sir Hubert HULL, 1949–1950
J. D. CASWELL Q.C. 1951–1959
Sir Walker KELLY CARTER Q.C. 1954–1971
Percy LAMB Q.C. 1959–1969
Sir Norman RICHARDS Q.C. 1963–1978
Sir William STABB Q.C. 1969–1985
Edgar FAY Q.C. 1971–1980

Lewis HAWSER Q.C. 1978–
John NEWEY Q.C. 1980–
David SMOUT Q.C. 1983–1987
Esyr LEWIS Q.C. 1984–

John DAVIES Q.C. 1984–
James FOX-ANDREWS Q.C. 1985–
Peter BOWSHER Q.C. 1987–

NOTE. Down to the coming into force of the Courts Act 1971, on January 1, 1972, official referees were appointed as such under powers conferred by successive Judicature Acts. Since that date appointments have been of "circuit judges nominated by the Lord Chancellor to deal with official referees' business" and those listed above since that date are the permanent London official referees so appointed. This list does not include the part-time provincial official referees.

# Appendix F
# Statistics

TABLE 1

Number of cases brought in, and number of cases tried, per year

**F–01**

| Year | Cases brought in | Cases tried |
|---|---|---|
| 1880 | 106 | 77 |
| 1890 | 267 | 208 |
| 1895 | 211 | 164 |
| 1900 | 337 | 242 |
| 1905 | 240 | 195 |
| 1910 | 207 | 166 |
| 1914 | 262 | 134 |
| 1918 | 120 | 84 |
| 1921 | 507 | 296 |
| 1925 | 270 | 168 |
| 1930 | 241 | 105 |
| 1938 | 261 | 202 |
| 1948 | 390 | 258 |
| 1950 | 438 | 289 |
| 1955 | 387 | 302 |
| 1960 | 220 | 154 |
| 1965 | 307 | 79 |
| 1969 | 376 | 63 |
| 1970 | 493 | 91 |
| 1971 | 440 | 94 |
| 1972 | 465 | 77 |
| 1973 | 510 | 98 |
| 1974 | 600 | 98 |
| 1975 | 739 | 112 |
| 1976 | 633 | 155 |
| 1977 | 691 | 119 |
| 1978 | 638 | 125 |
| 1979 | 625 | 127 |
| 1980 | 758 | 114 |
| 1981 | 870 | 112 |
| 1982 | 792 | 109 |
| 1983 | 901 | 151 |
| 1984 | 863 | 140 |
| 1985 | 1031 | 152 |
| 1986 | 1105 | 138 |

NOTES
1. Source: the Civil Judicial Statistics, H.M.S.O.
2. The difference between cases brought in and cases tried is almost wholly accounted for by settlements. Note the increasing ratio of settlements to trials in recent years.
3. The work of provincial official referees is not included.

## Table 1A

Cases commenced by writ marked "Official Referees' Business"

F–02

| Year | Cases |
|------|-------|
| 1982 | 12* |
| 1983 | 175 |
| 1984 | 201 |
| 1985 | 319 |
| 1986 | 320 |

* The procedure came into force on October 1, 1982

## Table 2

Number of Summonses heard per year

F–03

| Year | No. of summonses | Year | No. of summonses |
|------|------------------|------|------------------|
| 1950 | 1,206 | 1977 | 1,726 |
| 1955 | 1,158 | 1978 | 1,977 |
| 1960 | 774 | 1979 | 1,820 |
| 1965 | 800 | 1980 | 1,956 |
| 1969 | 952 | 1981 | 2,204 |
| 1970 | 1,223 | 1982 | 2,426 |
| 1971 | 1,226 | 1983 | 2,671 |
| 1972 | 1,136 | 1984 | 2,905 |
| 1973 | 1,231 | 1985 | 3,190 |
| 1974 | 1,398 | 1986 | 3,600 |
| 1975 | 1,608 | 1987 | 4,069 |
| 1976 | 1,423 | | |

## Table 3

Number of arbitrations brought in per year

F–04

| Year | No. of arbitrations | Year | No. of arbitrations |
|------|---------------------|------|---------------------|
| 1935 | 2 | 1976 | 3 |
| 1938 | 1 | 1977 | 2 |
| 1948 | 2 | 1978 | 2 |
| 1950 | 2 | 1979 | 3 |
| 1955 | 1 | 1980 | 0 |
| 1960 | 0 | 1981 | 0 |
| 1965 | 3 | 1982 | 0 |
| 1970 | 0 | 1983 | 1 |
| 1971 | 0 | 1984 | 0 |
| 1972 | 1 | 1985 | 11 |
| 1973 | 2 | 1986 | 19 |
| 1974 | 2 | | |
| 1975 | * | | |

* The figure given in the Judicial Statistics, 1975, Cmnd. 6634, is 21. This is clearly erroneous; the correct figure is probably either 2 or 1.

# Index